Stories From the Heart of Grit, Guts and Courage

Compiled by Kelly Falardeau

ISBN #978-1-989849-47-7

INTRODUCTION

Life is a journey full of twists and turns, where unexpected challenges often arise, leaving us feeling overwhelmed and helpless. These are the moments that truly test our strength and resilience, revealing the depth of our character and ability to overcome the toughest of obstacles.

It is by facing these difficulties head-on, with grit, guts, and courage, that we emerge victorious, stronger and more determined than ever before.

The authors of Grit, Guts, and Courage, understand the value of resilience and the impact it can have on our lives. That's why we're committed to empowering individuals to unleash their natural resilience and face any adversity that comes their way.

By sharing powerful stories of successful people who have triumphed over incredible odds, we aim to inspire and motivate people to find their inner strength and take control of their lives.

Kelly Falardeau invited the authors to share their stories because she found their stories inspirational. Ones of grit, guts and courage to persevere through life even though it can be full of challenges.

Kelly says.... It takes **grit** to get through those challenges in life, it takes **guts** to make those hard decisions and it takes **courage** to persevere through life.

TABLE OF CONTENTS

A Story of Grit, Guts and Courage and Following One's Passion

By Kelly Falardeau

Tell Us Your Story

Where do I start? I think the biggest start would be me getting burned as a two-year-old. We lived on a farm and my cousins were throwing shingles in the fire, and a spark came out and landed on me. I ended up getting burnt to 75% of my body, initially spending four months in the hospital. Then every two years until I was twenty, I'd have to go and spend another month in the hospital having reconstructive surgery. Growing up, I never thought I'd ever have a good life. I was teased, bullied, and shunned. I was picked on and called the ugly Scarface girl. It was a good thing that I was half deaf, because I didn't hear a lot of what the kids said, but I never really knew where my life was going to lead, until one day, I went to a women's event.

I had a different business at the time, and I was really struggling with my marriage. I was finally starting to realize that my marriage was toxic. I was in a dead-end job that I absolutely hated, but when I went to this woman's event, I met this lady who said I needed to sell that business and become a speaker. I said, what? I'm just a burn survivor, but she said no, people will be so inspired by your story. Now, at that time in my life, I was realizing that I wasn't in love with my husband, and I wanted to somehow end my marriage, but I didn't think that that would be an option for me because I had three kids. I didn't see myself as being inspirational, but she saw something in me that I didn't, so I went home that night and I said – to my now ex-husband - I'm going to be a speaker. He asked how I was going to do that, and

I said I don't know, but it's going to happen. That night, we were talking about it and he was telling me all these reasons I couldn't be a speaker; we were almost bankrupt, I wasn't successful, I didn't have a store, I wasn't Anthony Robbins, and I wasn't Oprah Winfrey. I wasn't anybody like that. When he says I just don't understand it. And he says, I don't understand why you think or how you think you can be a speaker. He says, 'I'm not trying to be negative, but I think you've picked a hard choice.' I just said, I don't know how, but it's going to happen. So that was the start of me becoming a speaker. I sold that business and became a speaker. I gave my husband half of the money, laughed, left the marriage, and moved in with my aunt and uncle. Then I had to deal with my job, because I had a full-time job at that time too.

My boss pulled me into the office and said I have a decision to make; my performance review was horrible. It was the worst performance review I've ever had in my life. She said you've got to think about this; are you going to be excited to come to work on Monday? Or relieved if you don't have to? That question hit me right to my core. I knew I wanted to be a speaker full time, but I had just left my husband five months earlier, so I didn't have his income to support me. Now she's asking me to quit my job and I'm living in the basement of my aunt and uncle's house, and I've got three kids. I'm thinking, how am I going to survive if I don't have a husband, a house, or a job? I went home that night, and I was looking through Businesswomen's magazine. Every second page said, 'follow your passion full time', and I flipped the page and it said, 'follow your passion full time' and then I came to the middle and a big black banner said, 'you are not trapped, God will provide you everything you need.' I go into work the next morning and I hear that little voice again say to me, are you going to be excited to come to work on Monday, or relieved if you don't have to? And I knew the answer; I would be relieved.

I sent my boss an email saying, 'you are right, and today is my last day.' I packed up my office, went home, and now I have a documentary about my life story, and I'm an eight-time best-selling author. I travel around the world sharing my story of being a burn survivor. All this happened because I trusted myself and I listened to my heart. The question about being excited to come to work, or relieved to not have to be the biggest turning point in my life.

How Did You Get Through Those Challenges?

It was really quite interesting because when I was living with my uncle, they didn't have internet, so as my business was based on the internet, I would get up at 5:30 in the morning and go to my ex-husband's house. I would get the kids up in the morning because he had to be at work at 5:30, so I would be with the kids and work there, or I would spend all day at Starbucks working. I also got a mentor involved. While my ex was telling me I couldn't do it, there were people popping up in my life that said this is your passion. You need to be a speaker, and you need to write a book. I really relied on my family and my friends to help me with the kids so that I could then follow my path and do what I needed to do.

What Would You Tell Someone Going Through a Similar Situation?

Ask yourself that question; are you going to be excited to do this or are you going to be relieved if you don't have to? That question was huge for me. I didn't realize how much of an impact that question would have on me. And I've even asked myself that question other times when I had to make a decision about something. The problem is a lot of times we don't want to do it because we don't know whether the universe is going to provide for us, so we're too scared to take that step and we're worried about people judging us. We're worried about not having enough money. All these beautiful things that happened to me happened because I quit my job and became a speaker full-time.

What is the Gift?

I don't think I would have stayed in my marriage or my dead-end job. I wouldn't have had all these beautiful things happen to me. I wouldn't have been able to go to Africa and help the kids there, and I probably wouldn't have a documentary about my life story. I don't think that I would have pushed myself as hard. In fact, that's what one of my coaches said. She said, 'I think if you had a man in your life, you wouldn't be working this hard, and you wouldn't be pursuing your passion because you'd be focused on the relationship.' The funny thing is when I lost my husband 12 years ago, I only had two boyfriends in the whole 12 years, and I dated a lot. But then I would go through phases where I didn't want to date. And then I remember saying to myself, I just know it. I'm finally going to find the man when my kid turns eighteen and they don't need me so much anymore.

Sure enough, that happened. It's been so cool to just give myself that time to pursue my passion and become a speaker, a bestselling author, and now coaching people to write books. And now I can also focus on having the relationship too. When I left my husband, I felt like I was being a bad mom. And I coined the term bad mom syndrome because I felt like I was traveling a lot, and I wasn't always home for my kids. I felt like I wasn't able to give my kids as much as they needed. But what was fascinating is that just a couple years ago for Mother's Day, my son gave me a letter, and the letter was all about how he hopes that he can be even half the person I am. It was probably the best Mother's Day gift I've ever had was a letter from my eighteen-year-old son. I still remember this other time when I was driving my other son to school, he said mom, my friends often complain about their moms, and I say to them, I can't relate. I'm so proud of my mom. I love my mom. And again, another moment when I was struggling with bad mom syndrome and trying to do the best that I could do being a single mom and an entrepreneur too. You don't always have money for everything. As an entrepreneur, you have to put money into your business, but you also have to put money into your kids. In the last couple of years when COVID hit, I lost all my speaking gigs, but this made me go into coaching people to write books and become bestselling authors, so the last three years have been my best years financially ever.

Words of Wisdom

Never give up, and if you have a passion in life, go for it. Even if you've got your husband or family members telling you it's not the right thing for you. Go find a mentor that is going to help you. That's what really helped me, I stopped listening to my husband and I started listening to my mentors who said there was so much value in my story, even though I didn't see it. I just thought of myself as a struggling burn survivor. The other words of wisdom I would give comes from a quote I came up with; ‘dreams are meant to be found, not tucked away in dreamland.

By Kelly Falardeau

https://www.KellyFalardeau.com

https://linktr.ee/kellynft

Kelly is a burn survivor since the age of 2 on 75% of her body. She found a way to go from near death to success, from the ugly scar-faced girl to the TEDx stage, not once but twice. A documentary about her life story, Still Beautiful launched on TV plus Goalcast launched a video that has over 10 million views. She is a full-time award-winning speaker and Best-Selling Author Strategist, coaching people to become best selling authors. Global TV announced Kelly as one of the Most Inspirational People of 2020.

To book Kelly to speak at your next event:
BookKellyToSpeak@gmail.com

You can watch her sizzle reel at:
https://www.youtube.com/watch?v=nV44doDQL3s

Unstoppable - From Wheelchair to Warrior

By Adrienne Nicole Tichy

Tell Us Your Story

In the quiet corners of an ordinary world, where life tiptoed through along predictable paths, a gripping tale of perseverance and determination unfolds - a story of triumph and faith emerges. At first glance, I appeared to be the picture of health; a tiny miracle welcomed into the world with smiles and laughter. But underneath this innocent facade, there was a stick of dynamite, and it was only a matter of time. The journey has been long and arduous, but I believe it is finally time to speak my truth.

When I was a little girl, I spent much of my time living in fear. At the tender age of five, I faced a life-threatening and life-changing ordeal - a 5 ½ hour seizure that sent shockwaves through my family. I spent a grueling three months in Jackson Memorial Hospital, an experience that would set the stage for health challenges to come. From that time on, my family and I wondered when the other shoe would drop. Although there were yearly doctor's visits and vaccine exemptions, my parents tried to raise me as normally as possible. Unfortunately, I was far from ordinary! By the time I reached the age of 20, I had already endured four surgeries and multiple hospitalizations. But it was an accident one sunny Sunday while playing co-ed softball that changed my life forever. As the runner tackled me, I flew into the air and landed on my side. My pancreas began swelling and enzymes started spilling into my bloodstream. Eventually the pain forced me to go to the hospital ER in the middle of the night, where I was diagnosed with pancreatitis. Since that pivotal moment, I have faced adversity head-on, enduring over 200 hospitalizations, surviving two comas, and spending three challenging months in Hospice care. Despite the severe toll illness had on my body, essentially leaving me disabled, I refused to surrender to my circumstances. Lying on the couch numbing the pain with narcotics for the rest of my life was not acceptable to me. Instead, I made a choice to continuously push myself beyond the limits my body was trying to impose. When, I could no longer absorb food in the traditional way, I was taught by the medical community to infuse IV nutrition (TPN) for 12 hours every day. My house started to look more and more like a hospital, but that didn't slow me down. In fact, I retrofitted a purse backpack to be able to take my TPN on the go. This allowed me to go about my daily activities with as much normalcy as possible.

Throughout this journey, one thing became abundantly clear - nothing can keep me down for long! With each new symptom that emerged, I embarked on a quest to find solutions that would allow me to participate in society as much as possible. Adaptation became my mantra and I refused to let my health dictate the boundaries of my existence. Quality of life is important to me. My ongoing struggle with malabsorption was a relentless adversary, causing my weight to drop to a dangerous 76 pounds. It was a frightening low point, one that tested my resolve like never before. As my muscles deteriorated, I became weaker and weaker. My world had become soooo small, as I could barely walk because it took too much energy to move about on my own. It was one of the darkest times of my life, and that is saying A LOT. I spent most of my days feeling stuck in my house, watching time slip away. I was envious of people who came to visit me because they could leave at some point. I felt trapped in my body with nowhere to turn. In a bid to regain some independence and mobility, my husband bought me the best gift EVER - a motorized wheelchair called a Zinger. The freedom it afforded me is difficult to put into words. I was **finally** able to participate in activities I had long missed out on, simple things like walking my dogs with my husband. One of the most memorable experiences was a cruise I went on in 2019. As I navigated the ship's floor plan, I marveled at how this chair had expanded my horizons and given me a chance to explore the world.

How Did You Get Through It?

I persevered through all my daunting situations thanks to the unwavering support from my family and a deep connection with God. I'm certain that God has kept me alive and has been with me every step of the way. The unconditional love I received from my mom, dad and husband was life-sustaining. Despite having a robust support network, I still struggled with the isolation critical illness often can bring. During quiet hospital moments, I turned to meditation and journaling for solace and reflection. I often brought my laptop so I could continue working! Patience and perseverance were formed in the crucible of those extended hospital stays. I also learned to grant people grace, recognizing that few could truly fathom the depth of my experiences. Amid it all, I cultivated resilience, discovering that the human spirit can endure and adapt in remarkable ways. Of course, there were countless moments of doubt, pain and uncertainty. I'm no saint! I often wondered what my ongoing battle with illness would mean for my ability to make a living and contribute to society. I also questioned whether a man would even want to marry me with all of my health issues. In a remarkable twist of fate, I realize now that everything I went through has uniquely qualified me for the challenging work I do now. Who better to help people recover than someone like me who has recovered many times over?

What Would You Say to Somebody in a Similar Situation?

First, I would suggest getting a support system up and running as fast as you possibly can. We aren't meant to do these things alone. A lot of times people feel like they're the only one with these problems, so get yourself a stellar support group. They will be able to help you through in ways that others can not. Be conscious of your attitude as well, holding onto hope as tightly as you can. Then I would say learn about your specific condition from your doctor, physical therapists, or other medical professionals. Resist the temptation to over research and self-diagnose but trust your gut. Someone graduated at the bottom of their class in medical school, and you **don't** want those physicians. Get second and third opinions if necessary and consider going to a teaching hospital. You could also cultivate a relationship with a higher power, somebody that you feel you can turn your health and your life over to. It can be difficult to understand why this is happening to you, so it is important to express those emotions. Just don't go overboard and monopolize the conversation! Help as often as you are helped.

What is the Gift?

The gift has been to see the silver lining in every situation. A lot of times we go through a situation, and we feel like it can be a tragedy. But then when we really look back at it, we see there's a gift in it. I think that every experience that I've had has the person I am right now. I can't tell you how many times my mom said that she wished she could have kept me from playing softball that day, but I told her it wouldn't work anyway. You can't change one thing without changing everything about who I am right here and now. It's given me the gift of seeing things from different perspective as well. For example, when a nurse is trying to get blood out and is failing miserably, I can choose to believe she is an evil human being, or I can decide to give her the benefit of the doubt.

Words of Wisdom

Where there's breath, there's hope. There are many times I wanted to give up, so many years where my life was threatened. Nobody has gone too far down the road that they can't be healed or helped. Sometimes we just need to let others hold sacred space for us when we are hurting, or have some type of a critical illness, including addiction. We can all be a little less judgmental and give a little more grace, because we're all recovering from something. My Near-Death Experiences (NDE) have also shown me that there is more to life than what we see with our eyes. I got a glimpse of heaven that few are afforded, and I know what is waiting for me on the other side. I truly believe that my soul chose this existence, and I just need to walk through it by taking the next right step. I know we are all here to help people save and change their own lives. Is it finally your time?

What Kind of Work Are You Doing Now?

My husband Jim and I created a Recovery Residence Community called The Lodge at Delray Beach 15 years ago in our hometown. We can accommodate 15 men who are just out of treatment for drugs or alcohol. We are known around town as champions for the marginalized. A lot of times we are the last house on the last block for people deep in their addiction. We've also launching our online, 12-month program called 'Recovery Comes Home' in early 2024. We walk through the first year of recovery with the client in the privacy of their own home. If someone can make it to a year, they have an 80% chance of making it long term. But if they don't make it to that year, the statistics drop to only a 15% chance. We're bringing recovery into people's lives to help the 80% of people leaving treatment that don't come to a facility like ours, and just go back home.

By Adrienne Tichy www.TheLodgeDelray.com

Unveiling Resilience: A Journey of Healing and Empowerment

By Anna Ditchburn

Tell Us Your Story

Before I start, let me warn you that my story touches on some tough subjects. It was a difficult journey for me, but I'm sharing it because I know there are people out there who need to hear it. My hope is that my story helps you see that even when the night is darkest, the dawn will come. Imagine a four-year-old girl watching her dad walk away, not knowing he'd never return. That was me, living in Russia, with a young mom left to fend for two little kids all by herself. Those early years were cold in more ways than one. On some nights, we couldn't afford to keep the lights on, and my mom's lullabies were our only comfort. As she sang, her voice whispered, "Even in darkness, we can find a glimmer of light."

Six years later, our knight in shining armor arrived - my stepfather - and we thought finally we have support, we have a provider, we have a man in our family. Just a few weeks later, he revealed his true face. He was an Army guy, very disciplinarian and very abusive both verbally and physically. My brother and I quickly learned how to walk on eggshells and obey all the rules; it was like living in the army in our house. We were beaten for everything. Because we were late, or because we had some clothes on the floor, or because we didn't clean properly enough. My mom didn't stop his tyrannical parenting because at that time, it was very shameful for women in Russia to be single mothers. So she gave him all the power to do everything he wanted. When I turned fifteen, the physical and mental abuse turned into sexual abuse. He sexually abused me for nearly six years - from fifteen to 21 - which resulted in two pregnancies and forced illegal abortions, damaged my reproductive system. When I wanted to become a mom - which was my most cherished dream - I had some challenges. I had nineteen consecutive miscarriages, including three ectopic pregnancies. When the sexual abuse started, he threatened my life, as well as my mom's and my brothers live. Knowing how abusive he was, I believed him. At the age of twenty-one I realized that I couldn't do this anymore, because carrying this secret and the shame is a very lonely and dark place. So, I ran out of the house. I've been carrying all these fears, shame, guilt, pain, and loads of anger towards him for nearly twenty years. Even though I looked like I had it all together on the outside, inside these feelings were eating me alive. It felt like a cancer - the longer I was carrying it inside, the bigger it grew. One day I met the person of my dreams – my husband – who made me feel so safe. Because of his nature, and talking about everything that he's gone through, it made me really safe to open up to him.

When you go through sexual abuse, you're carrying a lot of shame associated with that. Sometimes it's not even your shame, because you don't understand that. You might not be able to do anything at this point. When I opened up to my husband, it was the best moment of my life, and it felt like the weight of the whole world came off my shoulders. His reaction was the reaction I had always hoped for. He supported me so much as I looked back on those twenty years, and I thought why I waited for such a long time to free myself from the tyranny of the exhausting, negative feelings and emotions. He helped me to get into the healing, because I was so resistant to my healing. I didn't realize that this childhood trauma was haunting me for all these years, and it was coming out in terms of me wanting to be a people pleaser, and not being able to say no to people when I wanted, looking for external validation, not trusting myself.

It explained my perfectionism, workaholism, drinking, and all this stuff. When I finally realized what was causing it, I felt free.

I felt amazing, and I found my passion in life. Now, I've channeled that newfound freedom into a mission. I'm a coach and hypnotherapist committed to breaking the chains that tie people to their pasts. It's my life's work to guide others out of the darkness and into the dawn of a new day.

Did You Ever Go Through Feeling That No Man Would Ever Want You?

Have you ever felt invisible? Like you're in a room full of people, but you feel all alone? I know that feeling all too well. You see, it's not always about how you look on the outside. Sometimes, it's the battles inside that matter most. Our connections with others—be it family, friends, or partners—are a reflection of the connection we have with ourselves. You might think you need to be the prettiest or the best dressed. But trust me, the real magic is in the way you treat yourself and others—with kindness, love, and understanding. When I looked in the mirror, I used to see someone who was unworthy. Someone who thought, "Who could ever love this broken soul?" Abuse, whether it comes from others or from our own thoughts, has a sneaky way of stealing our light. There were times when I felt that the scars of my past made me undesirable. Like no one would ever truly see and love me for who I was beneath the surface. But I've since learned that true beauty and worth come from our spirit, our energy.

Today, I'm in the most loving relationship I could have ever imagined. But it wasn't always this way. I jumped from one relationship to the next, always wondering why they turned sour. Now I realize that I was repeating the cycle of what I'd seen growing up—a story of hurt and heartbreak. But here's the thing: We have the power to rewrite our stories. It took a lot of self-love, reflection, and inner work to get where I am today. By healing my own heart, I was able to attract the love and kindness I truly deserved. If my story speaks to you, if you've ever felt less than or not enough, I want you to know you're not alone. And more importantly, with a bit of self-love and patience, you too can find the love and happiness you're searching for. Don't let past shadows dictate your future shine. Let's journey to self-love together.

What Would You Say to Someone Going Through the Same Thing?

That's such a great question, because you know what? I've met a brave young girl who's been through that struggle, just like me. When I met Landon, we connected soul to soul. She was only eleven when someone she should've been able to trust betrayed her. She felt lost and shattered. I opened up about my own story because once upon a time, I was just like Landon—a young girl drowning in silence, aching for someone to talk to. I remember thinking, "If I can reach out and make a difference for just one girl, then it's all worth it." When I met Landon, our hearts spoke the same language. She knew I got her, that I felt the same shame, the same guilt.

"Why didn't I stop it? Why didn't I scream?" Questions like these haunted us both. But listen, I want you to know something important, something that saved me and saved Landon too: "It's not your fault." I couldn't change my past; I was stuck like a deer in headlights, conditioned to obey my stepfather's every command. The moment I spilled my secrets, it felt like the cage door swung open. For the first time, I felt safe and realized I wasn't alone. That's the precious gift I wanted to give to Landon. Landon found the strength to forgive—not just her offender but also herself. She's taken her story and turned it into a beacon of hope for others, sharing her journey on more podcasts. She's my hero, and she's her own hero too. So, if I could whisper just a few words into the heart of anyone going through this, they'd be: "You're not alone. I understand your pain, and there's a light at the end of this tunnel." What's crucial is to learn the hard lessons, to forgive and let go. And remember this—you can turn your deepest pain into your greatest power. I've done it. My suffering fuels my mission now, and it's the most fulfilling thing in the world because I know I'm helping others climb out of their own dark holes. I'm all in, sharing the roadmap to healing that I've scribbled through tears and triumph. I can't wait to help you find your way too.

How Can People Work with You and Get in Touch with You?

If my story resonates with you—if you feel that crushing weight and yearn to be free—reach out to me at Anna@AnnaDitchburn.com. There is nothing more therapeutic than to open up to someone who went through a similar situation, and who has been there and can be your support.

Words of Wisdom

Guess what? The world needs you. Yeah, you heard me right—YOU. You don't have to be perfect, and you sure don't have to be the prettiest or the smartest. You just gotta be you, because there's someone out there who needs to hear what you've been through. "Your story could be the key that unlocks someone else's prison. Don't be afraid to share it." You might think, "Oh, there are already people doing that. Why would anyone want to hear from me?" Well, let me tell you something. There are more than 8 billion people on this planet, and a whole lot of them are feeling down or dealing with tough stuff. At school, at work, in their families—people are struggling everywhere, every day. Your story might be the one thing that helps someone else say, "I can get through this. "Sharing your ups and downs, your wins and losses, makes you a real-life hero. By telling your story, you're holding out a lifeline to someone who's drowning. So don't hold back! Open up and say, "Hey, I've been there, and guess what? You're not alone. "Your words have power. They can lift people up and make them feel seen and heard. That's a superpower, my friend. Use it. Because when you share what you've lived through, you give other people hope. And hope is like a little light at the end of a very dark tunnel.

By Anna Ditchburn

Anna@AnnaDitchburn.com

https://linktr.ee/annaditchburn

Anna Ditchburn, a Certified Hypnotherapist and NLP practitioner, is a beacon of empowerment and healing for successful women who desire more than external achievements. With a past marred by systematic abuse, forced abortions, and personal loss, Anna's relentless courage and determination led her to reclaim her power and transform her life. Through her "Happy on the Inside" podcast and her unique expertise in Feminine Energy and Relationship Coaching, she inspires a generation to confront adversity, heal from shame and pain, and thrive like never before. Her fearless approach resonates deeply with those who are ready to confront their challenges and live their dream lives. Residing in Tampa, Florida, with the love of her life, Anna stands as a living testament to the indomitable human spirit, ready to guide you on your journey to fulfillment and success.

The Journey With My Mom and Her Sidekick, Dementia

By Bettina Maria

What do you do for People?

I help guide people in connecting to their true essence and to step into their potential. As a transformational guide, I am passionate about empowering others. I use a variety of modalities, such as Breathwork, Reiki, energy, drumming, sound meditations and more. I love seeing the transformation that happens for people as they start to pull back the layers and dive beneath the stories and their beliefs and see there is something else within. I am excited to see the growth that happens. I share what I have learned with others so they can find their way in moving from the limitations of their mind into the infinite space of their heart.

Tell Us Your Story

The story that I wish to share is a story with my mom and her sidekick dementia. For me, this has been a journey of courage and heartbreak, a journey of surrender and finding strength. I feel that dementia is one of the cruelest diseases that exist because there is really nothing that can be done.

You just watch your family member in this case, my mom - disappearing slowly, ever so slowly, particularly over these last few years. When she was first diagnosed, she had a difficult time because she didn't want to accept it. She kept saying nobody calls me, nobody does this, and I'd say Mom, I talk to you every single night.

I had my family as my witnesses that I was making a phone call every night to check in. Finally, after six months, I went over to her home and I said Mom, maybe there's something wrong. She tells me no, I write everything down and you're making this more than what it needs to be. I burst out crying and asked if she would agree to see a doctor - and that was the start of the journey over 12 years ago. After all sorts of tests, my mom was officially diagnosed in November of 2011 with dementia. At this point, she was still living in her own home. While visiting my sister in 2013, my mom fell down a flight of stairs in the middle of the night. She cracked eight ribs and broke her shoulder blade. After this, we decided she should be tested to check her abilities to drive as we were already concerned about her driving and she failed the test, coming in at thirty two percent capability.

This ended much of her independence as she could no longer drive. A big decision was made to sell her vehicle which she blamed myself and the doctor for conspiring against her. Another huge decision came five years later when it was decided to move her from her home, a decision she made. She wanted to be closer to me because she had tripped on a few things and needed a ride to the doctor or other appointments. Once a week, I would go get her groceries and bring them to her house. Before that I was picking her up and going to the grocery store, but this would turn out to be a two-to-three-hour ordeal as she would forget where things were and what she needed. I learned from this and instead decided I would pick up the things she needed. We started to look at some places where she could go and live, and when we were ready to sign the paperwork, she said no, I want to stay in my home one more Christmas. So, we canceled everything, and she had one more Christmas at home. Six months later, we moved my mom into her new place and now it was time to sell her home. Thankfully, I have many great friends that came and helped me organize for a garage sale, to move, pack her stuff and clean her house, a process which took three months. I remember when the house was empty and now sold, I sank to the floor and started crying, wondering if I was doing the right thing. I trusted I made the right decision for my mom to move out of her home as she was now in a place where she could be helped and assisted. I remember suggesting that someone could come into her home and live with her to help out, but she was absolutely insistent that NOBODY was coming to live in her home. She moved into what was called independent living as we did not have a proper diagnosis in regard to her needing additional assistance. My mom had high functioning social skills and scored high on the mini mental tests. In October of 2020, my mom had a fall and broke her hip, and was taken to the hospital. Due to the severity of the fracture and her dementia, she was in the hospital for over two and half months in the middle of COVID. At the beginning, I wasn't even sure if she was going to make it out of the hospital. I was told that my mom would need full-time long-term care and I was given full power of attorney as the doctor could see she was truly incapable.

I had to give notice to her current residence and wait until she was accepted by another facility that could provide the proper care for her. In February 2021, we moved her into her new care facility. Due to my mom's dementia and her thinking she can still do things on her own, she has experienced many "mini falls" which further affected her mobility and has led to a steady decline with her being mostly in a wheelchair. Since December 2022 to now, we have had four visits to the emergency department with the most recent fall resulting in a broken nose. I have said since the first fall, that my mom will continue to fall until she doesn't. Many times, my mom will ask when she can go home or where her stuff is. I tell her we have to wait a little longer as her leg is still healing, and her stuff is in storage at my place. She looks at me puzzled and asks why. I remind her she broke her hip which is something we discuss often. It has taken incredible strength, guts and courage to watch my mom slowly disappear. My heart feels like it is breaking open over and over and over. Making decisions now as her advocate, feels like a huge responsibility. This has been one of the hardest journeys of my life. Though the good news at this point is she still remembers who I am, which is amazing! Though a minute after I have gone, she doesn't remember that I was there. I believe although her mind doesn't remember her heart does.

How Did You Get Through It?

Surrender was a huge piece of it, and finding some humor was another piece. I remember when she was in the hospital and I was leaving one night and I said, goodnight, Mama Bear. She just looked at me and said, I'm not a bear. I was reminded of finding the humor in those small moments. Compassion is another piece, compassion for your own self. I am also going to relate this to trust. I feel like I have cried a million tears wondering if I was making the right decisions and choices for my mom and also in watching my mom struggle to know where she is and what was and is happening.

What Gift do You See in Your Story?

I remember when we didn't even know whether she was going to make it out of the hospital. I was laying in bed and asking for guidance and to help me find the blessings in what was happening. Now I can see the blessings as I learned about my mom's family history. I didn't know much of the family history prior to 2020. My mom's family were part of the three million people that were expelled from their country in the Second World War. So, in essence, their country no longer exists. It was really a gift that I was able to find out more of this family history, and what my mom had experienced and gone through as a child. Another gift was, I connected with my two aunts who were able to share their stories and what they had endured during the war time. I didn't even know that my Opa had been a prisoner of war. Another gift is to know that I am here to help and support my mom to the best of my ability and not beat myself up.

What One Piece of Advice Would You Give Somebody?

Remember to breathe. Many times, when we are going through tough and uncertain situations, we will hold our breath waiting for the phone call, waiting for the next thing, waiting to see what's going to happen. Seems like we are forever waiting. Also take the time for you. Take time to give yourself a treat. Allow yourself to have rest and a break. Sometimes, we can push, and we go, go, go, and the person that gets neglected the most is your own self. How can you give from that place when your cup is empty? So, number one is to look after yourself and remember to breathe.

In September 2022, I opened Essence Studio, a wellness studio at www.essencestudio.ca Essence Studio is a heart-centered space for like-minded and inquiring souls to gather, to learn and to experience. A space where we can evolve and become aligned with our true essence through a variety of classes, workshops and events providing an opportunity to connect and gain a deeper understanding of self. Also, I am working on a new book called 'The Giant Onion: Peeling Back the Layers for Inner Transformation.' Much of the content is the sharing of my own transformation and my journey along with the processes and tools I discovered. It was only when I decided to do the inner journey that I realized that my answers were inside. However, this was the scariest place to be because I didn't know who I was. And that takes grit, guts & courage! I am still learning and evolving. "Doing it scared" has become my personal mantra in learning to listen to the voice and guidance of my own heart.

Blessings!

By Bettina Maria

www.BettinaMaria.ca

www.EssenceStudio.ca

Bettina Maria is an International Transformational Guide, Creative Sound Artist, Intuitive Energy Alchemist, Certified Breathwork Facilitator, Reiki Master Teacher, Author & Owner of Essence Studio Inc. Bettina shares what she discovered in her own life journey as a seeker of inner transformation. Bettina leads with her heart and is truly passionate in empowering others in diving deep. Bettina has guided over 2000 students and clients in experiencing more joy, peace and freedom in their lives.

Bettina led Journey into The Heart Transformational retreats to Sedona, Arizona. Bettina currently guides a bi-weekly Heart to Heart live zoom call sharing wisdom, laughter, and tears with other like-minded souls.

Overcoming Fear and Pursuing Your Dreams

By Chuck Anderson

Tell Us Your Story

Being able to be a self-employed entrepreneur was something that I always wanted to do. I shouldn't say that it's not what I always wanted to do. When I was first starting out my career, what I really wanted to do was be an electronics engineer. So, I did that, and I was going down that path, and about three or four years into it. I realized no, this is not my dream. So, I started looking for other opportunities and I knew I didn't want to have another job. I got a paycheck every two weeks, and while I knew it was coming which was great, it wasn't enough.

I was always very interested in business, but I was scared to take the leap because of my parents. My parents were farmers, and essentially self-employed and in your own business, but you only got paid once a year. When we sold our wheat and everything else that came from the farm, we would get that big payday but that had to last the entire year, and often it didn't. My parents always told me I needed to get a good paying job and get paid regularly, because then I wouldn't have to go through the same struggles that they had. But I always wanted to start something of my own. I wanted the freedom. I didn't like someone telling me you have to be here at 7am and if you hit 701, we're going to be standing at the door wondering where the hell you are. I started looking around for businesses that I could start and run so I tried out a few things, but that's where the courage part really came into this. It became clear to me after going to all these seminars and trying different businesses on the side and stuff that I was going to have to do a sink or swim type of deal, going to the job and trying to do the business on the side. It wasn't really going to get anywhere, and at some point, I was going to have to let go of one of them. In 1995 I quit my job, and my parents hated every minute of that. I moved back to Vancouver, I went full time into my own business, and I have been self-employed ever since. We've had good years and we've had bad years, but really what launched me into that was finding the courage to let go of that job, because I wasn't going to be able to do both. The message I kept hearing from my grandparents and my parents was go to school, get good grades, get a good paying job when you get out of school, and then buy a house and then do all the things. That just didn't line up for me at all. There was always that tug of war between that desire to go and do it and that programming of listening to my parents and my grandparents every single day growing up saying that's not what you do. Part of the courage is the learning to let go of the job, but also to let go of those expectations of this is how you do it. I'm glad I did it, because I not only let go of that job and started my own business, but I've also got to do some really cool things like produce software.

I've also written multiple books which I never thought I would do, I've taught courses, I've led seminars, I've spoken on stages as a public speaker, and lots of other things that as a kid I never really would have imagined myself doing. Back in the day, I was fascinated by Tony Robbins and his infomercial. This whole idea of selling in this program and I was just so into it. I remember having a very vivid dream one night where there was a seminar with thousands of people in the crowd. I looked on stage and saw it was Tony Robbins, but when I saw the face of who was on stage, it wasn't Tony, it was me. I woke up instantly in a sweat and trembling with fear; that's not ever going to be me. I never needed to do that because I was so afraid of speaking on stage. It's kind of funny because that became my life where I did speak on stages, big and small ones, and now coaching people one on one; I speak for a living. But it was very interesting at the time because it was so far from my reality, and it translated into a nightmare, which is today one of my best gifts.

I was not a natural speaker. I dreaded speaking, I hated it, and then you get all the feedback afterwards. I think that added to my anxiety, and I didn't want the criticism. I didn't want people telling me that sucked. All the things that I would hear throughout school when I was growing up, and that just contributed to more and more anxiety about it. The turning point for me was somebody said, you have a message to share, and you have information that other people desperately need. So, it's not about your fear. In fact, if you don't share that information with people who need it, not only is that keeping you safe and comfortable, but it's also ripping those people off because they need you and they need what you do. What I realized was it was about me looking good. It was about me presenting myself well, to the point where the audience said yeah, he did a great job, he was awesome. As long as I didn't screw up, I was fine.

So, all that fear and anxiety was about me trying to look good. What I learned from the words of that mentor was that it's not about me and it's not about how I look. It's about how am I serving that audience? How am I giving them information that's going to help their lives? As soon as I started to think about them, and how I was helping them and not about me and how good I was coming across and how good I was looking, the anxiety started to go away, because it became about service and not about looking good. That still serves me today. I still get nervous sometimes, but I just remember, I'm here to serve. There's a group of people here who need me today, so I'm going to show up for them.

What Would You Tell Someone in a Similar Position?

I'd ask them why do you want to do that? What you want to do is figure out if this is real. Is it just a random thought and you're going to throw everything away? Or is this something that's really calling; what is your why? What does it do for you? What does it do for your family? What does it do for other people? And if it's real, then I would say exactly what my mentor said to me. And that is, 'you owe it to the rest of us to take that next step and to put that out there, because we need your gift.' In today's world, we probably need it more than we ever did. We need people with amazing gifts and amazing talents to share. I would also say, surround yourself with support from people who believe in you and what you're doing. Then you're not going to be able to take the chicken exit, you're not going to be able to have your fear justify your lack of action. You surround yourself with people who believe you can do it and believe that it's worthwhile, and that's going to help you keep moving forward. Every time I raise the bar in my business, there's fear, I get scared, I have great friends who are also risk takers and also people who set a goal and go for it. We have each other's backs. And if you surround yourself with people like that, you got this and you can definitely do it.

What is the Gift?

The mindset that I've learned to develop says that everything that sucked has led me to something that's great. So, part of the gift is that belief, because now when something new comes up that suck, I ask how is this benefiting me? What's the bigger picture here? I think also being able, as a coach, to coach people through those feelings. There was a book that I read in my early 20s called 'Feel the Fear and do it Anyways.' At the time I read it, I didn't get it but I get it now. When you're feeling the fear, it means you're about to accomplish something great, something you've been asking for, something that you've been wanting to do. And so now I really check in with the fear and say okay, I'm afraid. So that means something amazing is about to happen. It's new, it's different, so it's triggering my fear response.

I would say that's the real gift, and hopefully, by leading by example, my four children get to see that. You know that they don't always do what I say, but I can see in them that they do what I do and what they see me do. I think to me that's the greatest gift;

if I can inspire them to follow their dreams and follow their path. I want to lead by example with the people that I get to work with every day in my coaching business, because I want to see people realize their dreams and help people overcome those hurdles. The other gift is gratitude and peace, because my childhood was anything but peaceful. I was bullied, told I was wrong, and told I was stupid. I was all these things. That's not peaceful. I even had to run for my life a few times from bullies. I still have that instinct sometimes. If I turn a corner, I check to see if there is somebody behind me. Today there is peace from knowing that I'm doing what I'm doing because I choose to do it, and I'm not forced to do it. The gift is really having the liberty and the freedom to be able to choose to do that, and to be engaged in work that I believe helps others. When I help others, I can be an inspiration, whether it be to my children or my clients or whoever. That's when I feel fulfilled. That's the gift.

How Can People Work with You?

There's a lot of ways that people can work with me, but first and foremost is to have a goal. If you have a goal - something that you want to do, or something you want to build - then reach out and I want you to tell me about that goal. I want you to come and tell me what it is. Maybe you're trying to build a business. Maybe you're trying to get booked as a speaker on stages, or start a podcast or sell a course, or whatever it is you're trying to do, start with a goal in mind. Then connect with me and tell me what it is. If it's something I can help you with, then I'm going to help you with it. If it's not me, then I'm going to connect you with one of my friends who can help you, because like I said before, we've got your back, we've got you covered.

By Chuck Anderson

www.Chuck360.com

Betrayal – Let It Empower You

By Debora J. Hollick

The Seven Stages of Betrayal

Disbelief.

Shock.

Violation.

Anger.

Decision

Acceptance.

Forgiveness.

These, I have found to be the emotional stages of being betrayed, personally and in business.

Is The Act Of Betraying Someone A Deliberate Action?

I Say Yes, It Is. It can be avoided. It has a profound emotional effect on the injured party, that more often than not, is damaging. Depending on the severity of the situation, it leaves one with scars that may not ever heal. This can be emotionally, mentally, physically, and spiritually. Writing About Personal Stuff Is Hard In oh so many ways! Wounds and vulnerabilities are exposed, yet again, making us susceptible to judgment, fear, anxiety, rejection, embarrassment, anger, frustration, and regret. And let's not forget, feeling stupid for some of the choices made along the way.

Which Do You Think Is Worse, Personal Or Business Betrayal?

I guess it depends on the person having the experience, or in my case, experiences. Lucky me, I've had two such life-altering opportunities to grow from. One might say, I really am the lucky one, as they may have had multiples.

Personal

In my early twenties, I was with a man twenty-three and a half years older than I. We were in a common law relationship for about three and a half years when we decided to move from where we lived a considerable distance away.

Truth be told, living together without being married, never did really sit well with me. Maybe it was the Catholic girl in me who always felt like it was a sin, and I shouldn't be doing it. We had discussed marriage on multiple occasions and decided that we would get married prior to the relocation.

Prior to him leaving, we decided to go and look at rings. He made an appointment with the jeweler, and we had a private showing of engagement and wedding rings. He wanted me to pick out the three that were my favorites. I did just that. He would choose the one he liked best from those. Even though we had made the decision to marry, a proposal was never discussed, so of course, I was full of excitement and anticipation, for if and when it would take place. We both wanted it to be special and didn't want to take away the surprise element. And when it happened, it really did come as a complete surprise! Enjoying dinner at home, he asked me to get him another plate. Not feeling like I really wanted to do so, I asked him why he couldn't get it himself? Afterall, there wasn't anything tying him to the chair! He finally convinced me to get up and get it for him. When I opened the cabinet, there was a small pastry box sitting on top of the plates. If you know me, you know how much I like my sweets, so, while laughing, I said, "What's this?" "I bought you a treat."

Appreciating his thoughtfulness and the surprise, I thanked him and brought the box to the table and set it aside while we continued enjoying our lovely dinner together. You guessed it! This was his surprise proposal. Of course, I said yes. He went on ahead of me to where we would be living due to being offered a very good job. I stayed behind to continue with my job, which was also very good, and plan the wedding. This was back in the day when long distance calling was very expensive, something to the tune of a dollar a minute, if I recall, maybe even more. That being said, he would call me at least once, if not three times a day, to see how the plans were coming along, provide his opinions and ideas and talk about our new adventure together.

During these conversations, he would express his love and devotion, how much he missed me, and how much he was looking forward to us being together. I think it was approximately a month prior to our wedding date when I decided it was time to quit my job. There were still many finishing touches to do for the wedding and I wanted some time off to spend with friends and family since I would be moving nine hours away. Visiting would only happen a couple of times a year, if that. I couldn't figure it out, but he was so angry that I quit my job! It couldn't have come as a surprise; we had talked about it. It wasn't long before it became very clear to me. Let me cut to the chase. HE WAS LIVING WITH ANOTHER WOMAN! There is a lot more to this story which, if you like you can read about in Mila Johansen's *Cinderella Monologues*, available on Amazon.

Business

I had someone working with me in my business, and while I couldn't put my finger on it, I kept getting this odd feeling that something just was not right. I had been running one of my businesses on my own for many years and was tired. I wanted someone to help me train my contractors so I could focus on growing the business. The person I chose, had worked with me for many years, had the skill set required for supervising and training others. She was eager to help me grow my business; at least that is what she told me. Although I had a bit of hesitation, I went ahead with promoting her to a supervisory position.

Perhaps due to my many hindsight experiences being 20/20, I have become a major proponent of *Listen To The Whispers Or...Get The 2x4!* - so much so that I wrote a chapter on it, in Corey Poirier's *bLU Talks, Business, Life, Universe, Vol 3*, which is also available on Amazon.

I should have listened. I should have paid attention to the red flags waving right in front of me. When I did the training and continued to work with my people, they stayed for many, many years, including her! However, when I turned them over to their new supervisor, they would quit within a couple of weeks! I was puzzled. Something felt off and it kept happening. Still, did I listen? NO! At first, the whispers were just fleeting thoughts. Three years went by. Yes, you read that right – three years! Over and over, I kept hearing whispers, getting a bit louder each time. I began receiving actual, audible transmissions that translated into words. "Fire her!" "She is sabotaging your business." Still, I didn't listen. I felt sorry for her and overrode, much to my chagrin, my intuition and guidance, the Universe was so lovingly and clearly giving me. Perhaps, some might think I'm not too bright.

Disbelief

In both of these instances, I just couldn't bring myself to believe that anyone would want to do that to me. It didn't make sense.

Shock

I guess it was too painful to fathom or understand at the time so, what did I do? I made excuses for the behavior, situations and events that were taking place right before my own eyes. Looking back, it seems it could have been so easy, if I just listened, trusted, and took the necessary action. It would have been inspired action.

Violation

In both cases, my trust was severely broken. How could it not be? Be it personal or business, when you place your trust in someone and they abuse you in this way, it can be very difficult to put yourself in that position again. The pain is gut wrenching.

Anger

Eventually, I came to terms with the first three stages and then I was angry! It's okay to be angry. It is how you choose to channel that emotion that matters. I chose to become empowered by it.

Decision

There is power in decision making. Here I was in both circumstances, faced with no choice but to decide. For me, confronting my ex-fiancé and ending the relationship was the only solution. You might be surprised to learn that he still professed undying love and devotion, even after he was caught! Uh, I don't think so! Businesswise, the situation was on the brink of being catastrophic as it almost ruined my business so again, the appropriate steps had to be taken.

Acceptance

What choice did I have but to accept things as they were?

I believe things happen for us not to us, and when I look back at both experiences, the benefits of ending both relationships were in my favor.

Forgiveness

For years I repeatedly berated and blamed myself. I took those hurt feelings and built walls around me so I wouldn't allow myself to be in that position again. It didn't serve me well. While forgiveness is the most challenging step, I've chosen to forgive them for their actions, although, in no way do I condone it. Perhaps, most importantly, I also chose to forgive myself. In making these choices, I freed myself from carrying the excess emotional baggage. If you find yourself relating to my story, it is my hope that you, too, will allow yourself to move through these seven stages and also, feel more free. Afterall, we are the sum total of our experiences. Let's allow them to serve instead of hindering us.

By Debora J. Hollick

Debora J. Hollick, The Smash Through Mentor, is a Speaker, Multiple International #1 Best-Selling Author, Award-Winning Productivity Facilitator and 12Trainer. She helps. businesses and professionals, smash confusion, solve chaos, and stop cussing, to optimize personal team performance and productivity. In customized sessions, Debora shares her research. methodology that is proven and has been presented globally, on how Thoughts = Performance. She is a dream builder and persistent sales wizard that has been there and done that. Debora speaks in person and/or virtually to Corporations, Groups, and Associations of all sizes. She is the author of LIVE LIFE IN W.O.W! Nuggets of Wonder, Openness Wisdom anthology book and is the founder of Look For W.O.W! events.

https://www.linkedin.com/in/deborajhollick/

https://www.facebook.com/SmashThroughMentor/

Debora@smashthroughmentor.com

An Outsider in Education Reform

By Diane Devenyi

Tell Us Your Story

In 1999, I attended a literacy training program thinking that I wanted to help my own children with their schooling and literacy education. When I stood up to introduce myself to 35 seasoned educators, I said, "I'm Diane Devenyi, mother of three, former tax lawyer and I'm here to revamp education on the planet." What?! It was not my intention to say that; I didn't even know what "revamping education on the planet" meant.

It was 1999, and nobody was talking about the planet. I remember sitting there thinking, "What does that even look like?" What I did feel in my bones, however, was that it was true. During the next break one woman came up to me and said that I was the only person in the room that really interested her. She complimented me on my commitment, saying that it was" like, a 20-year project". I recall thinking, "This isn't going to take me 20 years." So here I am 23 years later, still in the thick of things. It all began with my own education. Until grade three, I couldn't learn enough; everything they asked me to do–spelling lists, times tables, reading books–I would run home and do it all. By Grade 4, however, everything changed. On the first day of school my teacher and principal were trying to figure out what to do with me because I had already completed some of the grade six curriculum. I recall thinking that they were not interested in helping me find the best version of myself, they just wanted us to be the best at what they were asking us to do. At 9 years old, I was fully aware of the distinction.

From that day forward, I did only what was required to be the best in my class at whatever they asked us to do. I saw it as a game, but it wasn't fun for me. Eventually I really hated school, even though I graduated with the highest grades in my high school, went off to university on scholarship, quickly got into law school and was called to the bar when I was twenty-four years old. In my first full time job I worked in the tax department of a large accounting firm. It was intellectually stimulating but not my passion. I started having children, and when pregnant with my second son, I decided to take time off to be home with my children. As they grew, my "love for learning" juices started flowing again and I threw myself into learning more about school and education. I saw that there was a lot of unhappiness, and even though my own story hadn't encouraged me to want to change education, when I began volunteering in my own children's classrooms, I didn't like what I saw.

I saw parents and teachers who were overwhelmed, and children who felt like failures in a system that focuses more on our weaknesses than talents. This must have been brewing inside of me when I made the bold statement about "revamping education on the planet." About four years into it, I was doing pilot projects in Toronto schools and focusing on literacy foundation. It was exciting to see children having breakthroughs and feeling smart for the first time in their lives. It didn't take long, however, to see that education reform was not an overnight fix. The systems are huge and cumbersome with many layers of bureaucracies, egos and habits. Eventually my naivete wore off. I remember the day that I realized that the work I was doing was not going to benefit my own children – but I was determined that it would benefit my grandchildren. I had experienced some pushback about the fact that I was an "outsider" to the education system. It was true: I had never been a classroom teacher but as a parent volunteer and project provider, I had seen the struggles from every perspective and I understood the pressures teachers were facing to meet diverse needs, expand curriculum as technology was growing and add increasing reporting tasks. I also wanted the freedom to design new programs that would truly improve the experience of school and find the hidden genius in every student. In 2005 our Premier suggested that I return to school to study education and offered to write a reference letter for me. So, I returned to the same university where I had earned my law degree 21 years prior. I confirmed that there was a lot of confusion about teaching literacy. I also learned that Thomas Kuhn, who wrote "*The Structure of Scientific Revolutions",* described why major shifts in paradigms could not come from within the academy. Yes! I would be the outsider to shift literacy education. Over the years I have had a lot of setbacks, but I have never wavered in my vision. Lockdowns that occurred during the Pandemic confirmed that education needed to change. I keep taking it one day at a time. In 2020, my first grandchild was born, and I thought, "It's twenty years later, I have a grandchild, and I haven't changed education on the planet yet". I remember this little voice saying in my head, "Grandma, you promised that you'd take care of education for me. I'm here, so get on with it!"

Yes, it's been a roller coaster ride. It's been crazy. If I could start all over, I may have been more efficient at getting to where I am now. But I will never give up. I invite you to think about passions you have, Ideas about how things could be better, messages about creating a better world. Spend time contemplating and then dream about a different reality. Listen to that small voice inside, with your heart as your guide. For me, it wasn't enough that I hated school. I waited until my son hated school. You never know what is going to be your trigger. The sooner you find it, the better for all of us. Then start taking steps. Boldly. Consistently. Because my ideas are a threat to huge systems, while I have been committed, I also procrastinated. A lot. I have feared being ridiculed by or a target of those who feel threatened by me. It wasn't until my grandson's arrival pushed me to get on with my vision that I feel the fire of urgency.

What drives me is that I want every single person to know how important they are, and that they have everything they need to create a spectacular life of love and light. The best thing that can happen to humanity is to have every person find what makes them come alive, and then fully express that. That's the highest purpose of education.

What Do You Do for People?

Today I run The Secret Genius School to help children and adults remember our love for learning. I also created AHAssessments, which not only find hidden blocks to learning and literacy, we also reveal hidden talents and then use those talents to recreate new, seemingly impossible stories of success. Together we immerse in hands-on collaborative experiences and come out with confidence, curiosity, creative problem-solving skills, connection and joy. It's never too early or too late. My oldest student so far was 77 years old. He couldn't believe how happy he felt. My first book in a series I am writing about literacy and learning is already making waves among parents and educators. It's called "*Dear Genius, Harness the Hidden Power in Your ABCs for neater writing, better spelling, faster reading and turning thoughts into words*". Yes, it's a mouthful and it lists the common issues that can be resolved when there's certainty of the alphabet.

What Would You Tell a Parent Who May Need Your Help?

If your child (and/or you) struggle with messy writing, poor spelling, inconsistent focus, slow reading or trouble turning thoughts into spoken or written words, look outside the box for solutions. Your child was born to learn; just not the way their teachers were taught to teach. Trust your child's path and find the right guide for them. Children born in this century need to learn how to learn with confidence and curiosity, and then be set free to pursue their passions. We can't even imagine how the world will be in 5, 10, 20 years, so learning how to unlearn and re-learn are critical skills. Children need to develop their humanness to their fullest capacity. Schools are not equipped to do that yet, but you can be a role model for them. (And we can help you!)

What is the Gift?

There's nothing better than seeing someone smile because they just accomplished something that they never thought was possible. Sometimes it's mastering the alphabet forward and backward. Or printing their neatest alphabet ever with no reversals. Or balancing on one foot and catching and throwing a ball. In these moments they are re-writing their entire life stories.

Many times, over the years I have wondered why I chose the path I did for myself. Why do I want to challenge the education systems? Why am I creating programs, writing books, speaking to groups and spreading my message? The truth is that I feel that I don't have a choice. I cannot rest until every person knows how brilliant and important, they are, and is contributing to the story of what it means to be a human from a place of love and gratitude. I know that inside every person is a unique talent, waiting to be shaped into a skill. But this won't happen if your experience of school had you feeling stupid, or isolated or unimportant.

Tell Us More About Your Book

"*Dear Genius, Harness the Hidden Power in Your ABCs*" is the first in a series I'm writing about learning and literacy. Most people believe that they know the alphabet better than they do, and for this reason, they would never suspect that gaps in alphabet foundation could be holding them back. I bust myths about intelligence, laziness, fine motor skills, and focus issues. I also describe the secondary issues that can flow from misunderstanding what's really going on. Issues such as low self esteem, bullying, bedwetting, headaches and stomach aches. There's a section for assessing points of confusion about the alphabet, how they may occur and how to resolve them. It's not complicated and important to understand. It's a shame that people pay a lot of money for in-depth assessments that give lots of information about what they've identified as a strength or a weakness, but don't lead to a solution. The assessment in this book shows specific issues that are simple to resolve. In the two-day intensive workshops that I offer, you can watch your handwriting change from one day to the next. And then your confidence soars. Everything can change and years of struggle and suffering can be turned around. I just received an email from a family in England with whom I've been working, and the mother said, "You have shown us in 4 months what five years of school failed to do." Your genius awaits to be discovered by yourself and the world.

Words of Wisdom

This is the end of a poem I wrote that is on page 108 of my book:

Stand up because you matter.

Without you, the world would be flatter.

And destiny's pattern would be missing a part.

You were born to make life your art.

So, start today to craft a new way.

I've got your back.

Trust me with your heart.

Love,

Your Soul

By Diane Devenyi

https://TheLearningForce.com

https://thelearningforce.com/products/dear-genius

Diane Devenyi is an author and advisor who is revolutionizing literacy and learning. Her career focus shifted from taxation law to education reform when her three children were young. As a volunteer in their schools, she was shocked by the lack of resources and training for teachers to meet the needs of every student. She spent several years studying and developing leading edge learning and literacy techniques, eventually founding The Learning Force in 2003. Today her Smarten Up! Experiences for families merge joy with literacy, learning and self regulation skills to prepare each person to thrive in our rapidly changing world.

The Language of Play

By Dinalynn Rosenbush

Tell Us Your Story

The underpinnings of what I'm doing right now, is really the story.

I started a podcast called "*The Language of Play*" which teaches parents how to get kids to listen better through connection and communication strategies. As a Speech-Language Pathologist, I regularly see many parents struggle with the same things. They wanted to be able to help their kids learn to speak and they wanted to understand what their kids were saying. They wanted to know how to help their kids at home, and *they wanted the kids to listen better and follow instructions!* Over the years, I've thought about it so many times. I wish I could share with parents how to implement some of the strategies that we have as speech therapists. What is the theory? What is the strategy? and, "How can you do this at home?" I know I struggled as a single mother at home, and the speech pathology continuing education helped so much in my home! It's not rocket science, it's just knowledge like everything else. I've had this wish to teach online, in my head for probably 10 years, but life is busy, and my biggest hurdle is that tech overwhelmed and scared me, plus, I didn't have business knowledge.

My road to podcasting was not straight! I had just experienced an extremely dangerous bout of late-stage Lyme disease which took me out of my work environment and all participation in life as I knew it. I was in bed for much of two years. Interestingly, I didn't end up doing a business focused on health, which of course was the track I had to go down: repairing my health. That is an enormous story. It was through that story that I started to think in terms of *"Just because I don't understand, doesn't mean it doesn't work."* That concept was what I needed to get well, and it became my mantra. I went through western medicine and got even more sick from the medicine itself. Then, I did integrated medicine, and then, Eastern medicine. When I was in Eastern medicine, I thought "this feels nuts and I don't know what I'm doing." I kept saying my mantra, *"Just because I don't understand, doesn't mean it doesn't work."* and *"Just because I don't understand, doesn't mean it isn't true."* I repeated these sentences as my health was rebuilding.

I read a lot of books! I realized I needed to do deep work in my personal journey. What are my fears? What are my deep beliefs? What are my deep values? What is it that I want? It's been a huge growth curve to figure out! Out of that came the belief that I can do some of these things I only dreamed of.

During this time of reading, I came across a book - by author Andrew Womack - and I read the one phrase, *"Your life is an exact replica of your thoughts, wishes and wants."* I slammed the book shut and said aloud, *"No, it's not!"* and then, I reopened the book wondering if I misunderstood? I reread it and I slammed the book shut again. I considered my mantra and opened my mind to: "*How can that be true?"* That brought me down an entirely different route, because I realized I have to change HOW and WHAT I think. For me, that was - the overall thinking pattern and belief system I had going on inside. That is where I put my effort and energy. In that process, I opened up to the concept that maybe I can start a podcast. I knew I loved coaching parents because I did that in my Speech Pathology practice for decades. But could I learn to do it online? Maybe I can write a course. I had to face my fears of tech, of learning a new field - that is entrepreneurship and business. How will I find the people that want what I can help with? Will anyone listen? Will people buy this?

The first struggle leads to courage for the next struggle, which leads to courage for the next struggle, and so on. So, even though

I was laying on the couch grumping, "What good is going to come of having Lyme disease!?" I would have never ever predicted the outcome that came! The courage, the guts, and the bravery it took for me to choose *what did not make sense to me*, grew more courage, guts and bravery for the next time I was unsure of myself. Getting well from late-stage Lyme disease, when life and death was in the balance, brought me to the place of willingness. I chose what didn't make any sense and followed my gut. What I learned from that, it built me up in a way that I could tackle the next thing, and now many more things have come along the way. Eventually, enough wherewithal grew within me, and *The Language of Play* was born. The learning and details from start to publish are many as is the business learning! When you jump into something that is 100% new, it takes grit, guts and courage, and it's taxing, even when you want it; even when you enjoy it.

How Did You Get Through It?

The first part of getting through late-stage Lyme disease was really learning how to rely on God and people. I spent my time in a lot of prayer, meditation, thinking about my beliefs, and my values. I spent a lot of time in that internal space within myself, in my spirit, to figure out "what is it that I am made for? What is my purpose?" So, that was a mindset change. I also had to voice my needs to the people around me.I grew up with the idea that you have to work first and then you have time for play. A huge shift inside of me was to realize that God made me, as I am, for a purpose, and part of your purpose is what you find joyful - not just doing work, not just productivity. The spiritual part was one big shift and then came another big shift. All this was a foundation for stepping into something different. I had to reach out to people to ask questions, to be vulnerable in front of people and to admit, *"I don't get this, I don't know this."* It is hard to let myself feel really dumb - because I've prided myself on being smart.

One of the things that happened with late-stage Lyme disease is that Lyme was in my brain and my spinal cord, causing inflammation. You are not smart when your brain is inflamed. You can't function. During that period of time when my brain was inflamed, I presented as if I had dementia, and I didn't really know what was going on. My children were starting to talk about, *"What to do with mom?"* I couldn't track the conversations around me, and it was serious. As I recovered, I expected that doing a business would be easy. How foolish! I resumed the old thought that "because I was smart" I will have success. But NO! Because of this, I have grown and faced voices of my past as well as many limiting beliefs within me. I needed to follow my coach who challenged me to do what I thought didn't make sense. (Return mantra) I learned to ask the questions and to be vulnerable without shame, and to be able to just become proud of myself for the growth rather than to think about my lack, has been a big change in mindset.

What Would You Say to Someone in Your Situation?

Open your mind and consider that what you know isn't the only solution. What you know, is only part of a great big pile of different options. Think about yourself as a learner and relax knowing that it's going to be as it's supposed to be. Pray and trust that the steps that are before you are already laid out, you just have to uncover them. The peace that comes from that, allows some healing. Choose courage to uncover unexpected ideas, even when they do not make sense. Prior to getting that mindset, I was grabbing on to, "HOW do I do it?" Once I relaxed, I accepted that I wasn't in control, I also opened my mind and opened my body to whatever healing source there is beyond my personal knowledge. A lot of healing happened. In addition, BELIEVE that there's going to be something good that comes from it, even though you don't know what it is. Don't spend all your energy trying to figure out what it is. Once I relaxed and said, "I don't need to know," ideas came differently to me. Be mindful of the words you say to yourself about your situation. Carefully choose what you believe. Do this by deliberate choice. Create your vision, make your next step, and relax knowing that it comes in its own time. Trust that the person or help you need will arrive. Be ready to receive it. I had this experience a month ago, where I fell down and broke my kneecap. I am waiting for it to heal, and I thought well, what is the good that came from this? All of a sudden, I have time to do some other things that I had been wanting to do. Believe me, I would never have chosen a broken bone! Still, it's here, so there's some silver lining somewhere to find! This time the silver lining is being loved on by my family. I am also able to do some things at the computer, because I must sit still for a while. I don't like to sit still, but now is the time for it. Finding the silver lining is a good practice to help you relax some during adversity.

What is the Gift?

There are three main gifts. The FIRST GIFT is the idea of reconnecting to God, to myself, to knowing, and to be able to trust differently than I had been. It had been more in my head. Now, I think it's sinking deeper, where I'm able to trust my intuition a little bit better. Believing and trusting that who I am and what I love was placed there by God has given me a new perspective. The SECOND GIFT was that my family showed up for me and loved me. That was amazing. To be shown up for, cared for, nurtured, and walked through to health. I was in a space of complete vulnerability. I do not know if I would have survived on my own had people not stepped in. My family showing up for me, nourished me in a way that built deeper inner trust, so I didn't feel so alone. The THIRD GIFT was the learning that I can -and should- get my thoughts under my control. So, if our lives are, "an exact replica of your thoughts, your wishes and your wants," we need to do some internal analysis! If we're not liking what we have, we need to dig into our thought life. It's a journey!

Words of Wisdom

I'll return to those same two quotes, one from a book and one from me. If, *"Your life is an exact replica of your thoughts, wishes and wants,"* and you don't like what you have, you need to pause, really pause, and consider what are the deeper thoughts that you have? What are the beliefs inside of you that you didn't know are there? The more time you spend in a negative thought wishing it wasn't, you're deepening and anchoring it, because your brain continues to relive the thing that you think about. So be careful what you think about and how you think. Get guidance on this! It is a tough road to walk alone. The support of someone who walked it makes all the difference!

Secondly, there is wisdom in opening your mind. "*Just because I don't understand doesn't mean it doesn't work or isn't true.*" That mantra has stretched beyond getting through illness. It's still a stepping stone, to help me get to my next steps. This mantra opens my mind to what is the potential. The possibility? The what-if? When your mind gets open, the next question becomes, "Who does know this?" which has forward momentum.

How Can People Get in Touch with You?

Email me at hello@thelanguageofplay.com and go to my podcast! "*The Language of Play.*" Listen in to learn strategies to teach your children to listen better, and of course, you'll get to know yourself better along the way.

I would love to hear from you!

By Dinalynn Rosenbush

hello@TheLanguageOfPlay.com

www.TheLanguageOfPlay.com

The Courage to BE and TRUST Where You ARE

By Donna Fairhurst

Tell Us Your Story

Have you ever lived in a place that wouldn't let go of you, or you couldn't let go of it! It seemed that fate just kept pulling you back over and over in different times and seasons of your life. Sometimes it was a choice, sometimes it was a blessing, sometimes it felt like a curse and yet through it all, your life revolved around it, good, bad, or indifferent. Pincher Creek is like that for me. I was born and raised in Southern Alberta and bypassed the town many times in my youth to go fishing and camping with family and friends, never realizing that later in life so many pivotal moments would occur there. It's a small quiet beautiful town nestled in the rolling foothills close to the US and British Columbia borders not far from Waterton National Park and Westcastle Ski Hill.

I must have passed it a hundred times driving west on Highway 3 or south to Waterton, hither and yon with family and friends, yet never driven into the heart of the town or its iconic Main St. I am an empath and a psychic medium. You would think the universe would have told me and warned me of all the tragedy and triumph living there would entail. Nope, not even a hint. I wasn't living from Sacred Soul/Self then. I always felt an energy vortex around that whole quadrant of southern Alberta. I was drawn to it like a moth to the light and still am. I moved there sight unseen with my then husband Art. He had just graduated and accepted a new job. We had to choose between two towns, Hinton to the north or Pincher to the south.

We lived there happily until we moved to Indonesia in 1980. We bought the first of three homes I would own in the area and our two children were born there. Friends from college were moving there at the same time and we made many more that are still dear friends nearly 50 years on. Like most people, my life has contained so much happiness and so much pain. I have often said I felt like a human yoyo to God and Pincher Creek. Like the town I always return to, I have had multiple near-death experiences that left me reeling and returning again and again, from earth bound to heaven held, over and over. I felt like a yoyo to God, a soul on a string rolling up and down with no choice in the matter. Only years later would I find the courage to tell the tales of never-ending, all-encompassing, love and peace on the other side as well as the "Angels" and "Others" who live both here and there simultaneously, supporting and guiding us with their love on the path we have chosen to fulfill our life purpose HERE & NOW.

In Pincher Creek I endured the loss of a second child I deeply wanted, the death of my father, leaving our treasured home, our beloved dog, family, and our best friends, to move across the globe, to Indonesia for 12+ years. Despite the pain of separation, the excitement of living overseas was incredible. That's another book in itself. Three years later we purchased a property in Beaver Mines, just west of Pincher Creek, as a summer home. The kids and I came home every year for nearly three months because I wanted my children to know they were Canadian first and foremost and grow up around their best friends from birth as well. Nine years later I moved there permanently several months after purchasing a friend's travel agency, enduring a bitter and acrimonious divorce, untangling all the crazy relationships attached to it, and finding what I was truly good at "the travel business." After all, I had done enough of it!

The summer of 1995 the area all around was hit with the worst rains and floods in a century. My little house on the mountain side was flooded out three times and the valley below looked like a lake with houses floating on it. It felt like my whole world was spinning out of control. Through it all I was working my way through terrifying depression, desperately staving off suicidal thoughts. I dumbed down the worst of the pain and disappointment in myself, and others, with anti-depressants and a lot of rum and coke. Not a great thing to do! I was tangled up in non-serving, very complicated, relationships. It was hard work living through all the upheaval, pain, and sorrow in a small town where everybody knew everybody. It took Grit, Guts, and lots of Courage just to get out of bed most days. I was pretty good at masking my crap. Life is a choice and has a way of moving on with or without you.

I loved my business and had great staff and loyal clients. After two years I decided to sell my home in Beaver Mines, invest the money, and take a four-month sabbatical to travel through Mexico and Central America with my daughter. I needed to get away from it all and have some space to pull myself back together. My son was happy working and living overseas in the Caribbean. I had no one and nothing to hold me back so we started planning.

A few months before our departure I met a man who would become a life partner for a while. He was a decent man, single, and living far enough away that he wouldn't be a nuisance, or so I thought, and started dating him. He became my Mr. Good Enough for right now. At the time he was trying to convince me it was true love in the making. I resisted because we were so opposite in nature, and I was going traveling. He in turn sold all he had in the city he lived in, showed up in Pincher Creek, and announced he was going traveling with us. We decided it would not be bad to have a man along because we would be going to some remote backcountry locations for significant periods of time. The trip was both grueling and glorious, uplifting, and magical, challenging and intentional. We visited every pyramid and spiritual sight we could in every city, town, and village in every country. We hiked, biked, canoed, bussed, and flew thousands of miles pursuing higher awareness. It was truly the awakening of my spiritual soul and the time when I accepted my visions, angels and guardians' voices as divinely guided. I learned to truly trust and live by and with my intuition from heart centered awareness, all the while staying in the Spiritualist Closet. We eventually had to return as Kim was starting University in the nearby city of Lethbridge. We stayed with a friend for awhile and ended up renting a house of a good friend, Susan. She had accepted a job in Calgary and wanted to keep her home in Pincher and come home most weekends. We needed a place to stay while we decided whether to rent or buy in Pincher Creek. Back to work I went, and Neil started a consulting practice. It is a beautiful little home with a gorgeous back yard that draws you in to enjoy nature and meditate. Spring was gorgeous, warm, and early that year. Susan came home one weekend and, as Neil was ill in bed with the flu, we decided to do the spring yard clean-up. It was such a glorious day, and we enjoyed every minute.

Towards 3 pm we decided to call it a day. My intuition had been screaming at me all day to go to Beauvais Lake. I suggested we grab a thermos of tea and a pizza and head out to enjoy the waning afternoon, a spontaneous picnic, and hopefully a glorious sunset against the backdrop of the lake and the Rocky Mountains. Most of the cabins clustered around the northeast end of the lake were still closed for the winter. There was a smattering of fishermen along the banks near the cottages and car park, and one other car parked half way to the southwest point of the little lake. There was a young man, Nathan, sprawled across the back seat of his parent's car reading. We could see the rest of his family hiking across the south end of the lake to everyone's favorite viewpoint.

The lake still had a lot of thin ice floating in it and the waves were increasing with the gusting chinook winds that always seemed to blow in Southern Alberta. We noticed a red canoe with two occupants moving slowly north toward the car park. It was difficult paddling against the waves. Susan remarked that it did not seem like an ideal day to be canoeing. There was too much packed snow for us to get further up the point, so Susan turned the car around facing back the way we came. As I broke out the pizza, I noticed Nathan jumping out of the car and running to the lake edge. He then turned in our direction and began running like hell, waving his arms frantically. A voice in my head said drive now! As we raced back around the point, I saw the canoe overturned in the lake a good distance from the shore. We reached Nathan and jumped out to assess a desperate situation. We all knew the water was frigid! No one could survive very long in it with or without a life jacket.

Both canoers, a big man and a very small woman were in the water. He was trying to swim to her, and she was floating face down in the water with a life jacket too big to hold her head out of the water. The wind and waves smashed up against the overturned canoe and it was swinging wildly. I knew that Nathan was a good swimmer as he had been in the Pincher Creek Swim Club in his early teens and taken life-saving lessons multiple times. "Susan", I shouted, "Run to the nearest cabin, break in if you have to. Phone town and Beaver Mines for help. Tell them we will need at least three ambulances, heat packs, hypothermia IVs. and warm liquids. Then call the hospital and tell them we are coming in. Grab blankets, towels, coats, anything you can see that we can use to warm up. GO!" "Nathan, are you willing to try to reach them with me? You'll have to ditch your clothes. We will need them when we get back?" "Yes Mam," he said, shucking off his shoes and clothes." "Ok then. I'll take the man; you take the woman. We have about 4 minutes to get there and 4 minutes to get back max! If you realize at any point, you can't make it, just head back to shore immediately. Get her on the bank and start CPR. Got it?" I questioned as I threw off my clothes and we ran to the edge to dive straight ahead. I had two seconds of hesitation as I shucked my clothes and remembered I was braless. I took a running dive into the dark waters, all the while praying, "Angels, Guides, and Guardians don't fail us now. You put us here for a reason so lend us your strength!" It was such a shock to hit the cold water and have the breath rush out of my lungs. I can't believe our hearts didn't just stop. I did not know at the time that I have a rare congenital heart condition. Just hitting that water should have killed me! Adrenaline and angels worked miracles that day. We both made it to the canoe in good time. The man had pulled his partner's head back out of the water and turned her on her back again, trying desperately to hold her and cling to the canoe. We pried them apart and started hauling them back to shore. Nathan reached them first, moving fast and well with the small lighter woman. I was hauling the heavy semi-conscious man and screaming, "kick, kick hard or die!" Susan watched anxiously back on the shoreline with towels and blankets.

Nathan made it to the shore, and with Susan's help, got the woman out of the water and started working on her furiously. I made it to the shore yet couldn't lift the heavier man out of the water. We were both too frozen to move. Nathan turned, saw the problem, and leapt back in to help get the man on shore. We could hear the wailing sirens far in the distance. "Nathan, help the man he's losing consciousness."

I jumped over to the woman who was unresponsive. Susan threw a blanket around our shoulders and both canoers as I rolled her on her back and continued CPR. "I think he is having a heart attack!" Nathan yelled. "Keep it going, don't stop!" I responded, all the while praying, "Dear God you wouldn't have brought us all here if you meant these folks to die. Angels, we need you now!" I felt an overwhelming sensation of warmth, Love, and Peace. I knew both Nathan and I were beginning to suffer from hypothermia and shutting down ourselves. Just a few seconds later the young woman jerked and started spewing water. As I rolled her on her side all five of us began to cry at the same time.

Susan moved in to try and warm her up, and I moved to help Nathan. Nathan's family arrived back and gave us all hot drinks from their thermoses as the ambulances arrived. I stood up cramped, blue, and shaking violently as the blanket around my shoulders hit the ground. I had forgotten I was naked from the waist up! Let's just say the Pincher Creek ambulance and volunteer fire department first responders saw me in a totally different light! All were polite and respectful enough of what had occurred that no one said a word to me, or anyone else about it, then or ever. Although one close friend was fond of saying to others with a wink and a laugh, "If you need to know the naked truth go to Donna. She'll save you."

As they loaded us all in ambulances and began the journey back to town, I remember saying out loud through shock and chattering teeth, "Dear God, am I done now? God laughed loudly, and my Angels sighed. "Not by a long shot, not even close! See you later!" was the voice only I heard. Thank God I couldn't foresee the future then to know what that meant. Both Nathan and I received Life Saving Awards for Bravery from the Alberta Lieutenant Governor, and the Keys to the Town of Pincher Creek. I admit that it truly felt like an honour we deserved. However, what I truly treasure is the ceramic angel the woman we saved sent to me after she was released from the hospital. She told me she had to send it to me because the first thing she heard was me praying to God and the angels. When she opened her eyes on the shore of the lake, she saw me leaning over her and a giant angel bathed in lavender light leaning over me with her arms and wings outstretched around us.

Life went on. 911 happened throwing the travel industry into turmoil. I reluctantly closed my agency, declared bankruptcy, and once again left Pincher Creek for good. Anyone want to place a bet on whether that was true and final for me or not? What I know to be true is there are no endings, just experiences that challenge us to lean into ourselves and be the hero in our own lives. If we can show up for others in the process, that is a personal choice and gift from God. The gift is in showing up, even if it means you might not make it yourself. That too is a choice. What goes around, comes around, one way or another. My husband Frank showed up in my life when I finally loved myself enough to be totally independent. I met him in Pincher creek in 1995 and ended up marrying him in 2006. Yup, you guessed it. I quit my fabulous executive job and moved back to Pincher Creek! If anyone had told me then that one day I would be married to Frank, partner in a machine shop and an antique business, train to be a millwright and a machinist, and love every minute, I would have thought they were nuts. In truth he is my soulmate and the man I finally deserved. His favorite saying is," To give a gift is to receive a gift!" It proved to me I should never say never again about a place or love. We eventually left Pincher Creek, moved around Alberta, and are currently living in British Columbia. We kept the house there though. You never know..........Namaste

By Donna Fairhurst

Donna is an Intuitive Life & Soul Transition Coach, Reiki Master, Psychic Medium, Empath, and Auric & Chakra Intuitive. She has studied spiritual & healing modalities and practices for forty plus years, embodies the highest degree of awareness, and is attuned to vibration healing, via combined Reiki, Chakra and Auric resonance. Combining psychic abilities, scientific aura imaging, and more, she empowers her clients to transition to their highest levels of personal awareness. As a Life/Soul Coach & holistic practitioner, she is

dedicated to raising the vibration of the planet one client at a time with joy, & purpose.

https://www.DonnaFairhurst.com

Overcoming Trauma, Finding Purpose, and Helping Others

By Dr. Barnsley Brown

Tell Us Your Story

I grew up in a good southern family in North Carolina. We were members of the large Presbyterian Church where the Governor and other prominent people went in Raleigh. We had a nice historic home in a very desirable section of town. Everything looked good on the outside, but on the inside, it was a mess because my father was not only manic depressive, but also using alcohol and drugs to self-medicate. I just remember growing up and thinking that he was always asleep, and I didn't understand why–He was passed out of course.

I love Christmas, and my brother and I always wanted my dad to participate with us in Christmas, but he was so depressed that he couldn't and wouldn't. I didn't really understand what depression was; I just knew my dad wouldn't come downstairs at Christmas. And so basically it was my mother, my brother and me; we were 'the unit' and my dad would never come and be a part of it.

My mother was really raging because she was dealing with two kids, and we were both precocious as hell. We were gifted kids, highly creative and eccentric, so she had her hands full. And then she had a third kid–my father.

My father was absent when he was there and sometimes, he was absent physically; there were times he would simply disappear for days on end and times that he went away to mental hospitals. I remember one time I was given a pair of leather boots, and that pair of boots was somehow supposed to make up for the fact that my father was going to be away for God knows how long in an institution.

I'm about to turn 57, and I'm proud of all that I've survived. I'm proud of the fact that I've made it to 57, because my brother did not. My brother died a couple of years ago. We had a conversation right before he died. I had the feeling that something was wrong, and I remember saying to my brother–his name was Eagle– you have got to give up this anger. He only wanted to talk about the past, all the stuff that had happened and all the ways my mother had been a raging, angry person. That's how she dealt with the situation.

My dad was an alcoholic and drug addict, and my mom was a rageaholic. She would hit my brother, who was always the rebel, and he would hit me, so there was a cycle of abuse and violence. My brother would rehash the pain over and over, which is why I said to him, 'You've got to give this up and forgive or it's going to kill you.' This was one of our last conversations, and he said, 'I know. I know Barnsley.' That was the last time I saw him alive.

The relationship was troubled between my brother and me because he stayed with my father when my mother finally left eighteen years into the marriage. She took me, but my brother wouldn't go because my mom was a rageaholic. My brother wanted to run free. He too developed a drinking problem, was diagnosed with depression, and had agoraphobia. There were a lot of things going on for him and he also had other serious health issues. He lived in a state of having so much potential that was so untapped in his lifetime. And also, he had a big heart. He was gay, and he won an award for his advocacy in the gay community. He started a food pantry for people with AIDS and even won a prestigious Volunteer Award from the Governor. He was very proud of the things that he did, but much of his potential was untapped.

I think one of the reasons I am who I am is because I've also gone through depression and anxiety. I had memories of being sexually abused by my father that only surfaced during COVID. I've been through a lot of stuff, but the way I'm able to keep smiling and moving forward is that I have had so much support, and I just want my story to convey to everyone that you've got to reach out for help. Thank God I got involved with Alateen when I was a teenager; Alateen is for teenagers who have parents or loved ones with alcohol problems. I also got involved with Al-Anon and then I got involved with Adult Children of Alcoholics, ACA. You can get meetings online so I can just tune into a Zoom meeting as I did earlier today. I've had counseling and therapy at times, also medication that helped me. I believe in all these things as a way to survive and recover.

I've also studied Reiki and I teach it. I've practiced it for over 30 years on myself every day. Reiki has given me a way to love myself; it's a very concrete way to give yourself self-love. I also know that in every piece of our lives, there's a purpose, and my purpose has been deepened by my own healing, by teaching others how to heal, and by helping women achieve financial freedom so they never have to stay in an untenable situation and can get the hell out. Whether it's in a job, a marriage, a partnership, I care about and have compassion for people who have been marginalized in some way, shape, or form. My compassion came out of my own experience of feeling like I didn't belong, wasn't heard, and wasn't seen when I was a kid. Most people would say now that they can't believe who I am, and that I write, speak, and share all this openly. But the truth of the matter is, my desire to communicate has been brought out of me by the experience of all the pain.

The point is, we need to reach out and get help. I've done all sorts of bodywork. I've given myself Reiki self treatments every day for over thirty years. I also go and get massages and acupuncture regularly. I've also studied and experienced all sorts of somatic healing. There's a great book, 'The Body Keeps the Score.' Whatever trauma happens to us gets stored in our bodies, so what we've got to do–if we want to have a life where we can smile and have joy and feel alive–is excavate that stuff and release it.

That's where teaching Reiki comes in, because my clients often say things like, 'I did more in that weekend with you In Reiki Level One than I've done in twenty-five years of therapy.' It really is a powerful thing to work with your body. We cannot just work with the issues that we've been through intellectually. We can't just talk about them. We need to exorcize them, get them out, and release them from our bodies so that we can be free! It's also a continual process. I have moments where I get triggered by something and I realize I'm not feeling safe, and then I'm able to look and ask 'Okay, what is this about? What age am I right now?' Sometimes I'll realize that I am three or some other really young age, and then I can do healing work to release that stuck trauma.

I just want to say to everyone, my journey is not one I would trade actually–I wouldn't trade any part of it. And I think when we're able to realize that everything we are and everything we've become is because of every bit of what was lined up in our life–what our soul chose to experience–that's when we're able to accept the journey for what it is and let go of any idea that things should have been different. So many people spend their lives wishing they'd had different parents, or wishing they'd had different experiences, or wishing that this or that thing hadn't happened. Well, it did happen. It happened, and yes it was awful. And there's no way to sugarcoat it. But there's a reason why what happened to you happened. When you excavate that and you hang on to that for dear life, then you can create your life's purpose around it. You realize that what happened to you has given you a divine calling. It's part of your vocation which comes from the Latin word 'vocare' meaning 'calling.' When you accept your calling, you stop questioning and start having courage. I love the word courage because it comes from 'couragio,' which means 'from the heart.'

And I believe that in our lives. We can say 'my heart is broken by this,' and yes, my heart is broken by a lot of things. My heart is broken by the fact that my dad was gay, but he had to be in a marriage. That was part of his depression; that he was gay and couldn't live that way openly. He also had a lot of different sexual proclivities, and he wasn't able to express those openly either. Perhaps if he had, he wouldn't have done some of the things that he did. He had to closet himself, which to me is super sad. I think about my mother with a man that she loved–she still considers him the love of her life even though they hated each other after the divorce–and not really having the love and desire coming back to her. Imagine being in love with someone who's gay, and not being able to have them really want you; it's just heartbreaking.

I can say my heart is broken by this, or I can say my heart is broken by the abuse I experienced in my intensely dysfunctional upbringing. I can say my heart is broken that my brother passed away and wasn't able to deal with the things that happened to us as children and let them go. I can say my heart was broken by ALL these things, OR I can say my heart was broken OPEN by them. My heart is broken open because now my heart has a place to hold other people going through similar experiences. My heart has a place for teenagers who are going through hell because that was the hardest time of my life. My heart has a place for single moms because I am one myself, I've been through that. My heart is broken open, not just broken. And I believe that when we can focus on that, then we will always be able to move forward with courage to fulfill our calling.

What Would You Say to Someone in a Similar Situation?

I would tell you that you matter. You are important. Reach out. Get on the internet. Look for Adult Children of Alcoholics and Co-dependents Anonymous; both free programs are open to anyone who's gone through family dysfunction. Look for a 12-

step program that will help you whether or not alcohol was involved. You could do Al-Anon, but Adult Children of Alcoholics (ACA) is not just for adults who are the children of alcoholics; it's for anyone who's grown up in ANY sort of dysfunction. People don't often realize that so I would say get on the internet, get yourself a meeting, and keep showing up. Also find yourself an excellent counselor and find friends who understand and don't expect you to be something you aren't, and who can understand all parts of you and your past and not feel sorry for you.

You don't need someone to feel sorry for you; you already know that. What you do need is to know that there are other people who've gone through and made it through, that you matter, that your voice is important, and you're going to make it to the other side of this. The challenge I would offer you is that when you do get to the other side of this mountain, you reach back and look to see who's behind you. Then help them come through what you have gotten through, so you all become ripples of positivity, love, power, and impact in the world.

What is the Gift?

The biggest gift is having my heart break open, but one other thing comes to mind, and that is that I'm able to see through all the bullshit on the surface. I'm able to see through what people say to what's *really* going on. I'm able to feel it even if they don't say it. I'm extremely intuitive–some would call it psychic–and I just download information and understand what someone is not saying because that's how I survived my childhood. I became acutely aware of what was going on with other people that was never voiced with words. This ability serves me now in my work, especially when I'm teaching Reiki. I'm able to pull trauma out of people so they can identify it and have huge releases, and I'm able to create a safe environment for people to do that.

Reflections

There was a moment in my life when I didn't want to be on this planet anymore. I was very clear that I wasn't going to hurt myself–I knew that–but I knew I just didn't want to be here anymore, and that was a wakeup call for me. That was a moment that I had to make a choice: Really, am I going to commit to this life and to work through the crap that I've got to work through? Or am I going to take an exit route? I chose not to take the exit route, and I would encourage other people not to take that exit route either. Reach out and remember you matter, and you are not alone.

By Dr. Barnsley Brown

https://spirited-solutions.com

https://www.youtube.com/@drbarnsleync

Dr. Barnsley Brown helps big-hearted women and business owners let go of the past and reach 6 figures and more, FAST with FUN through her business motivational presentations, kickass coaching, and transformational Reiki seminars. For over 20 years, she has trained thousands of people in Reiki in five countries worldwide and presented for over 2000 organizations such as the Environmental Protection Agency, Deloitte and Touche, e-Women network, Women in Networking, The National Association of Women Business Owners, Career and Technical Education associations, business centers, chambers of commerce, churches, non-profits, and many more. Dr. Barnsley is a sought-after radio and podcast guest and hosts the weekly Bold Badass Business Owners Show. Make sure you grab your complimentary copy of her e-book, 'How to Overcome Overwhelm in 7 Easy Steps, available at www.spirited-solutions.com. (Remember the dash!)

Collecting True Friends: The Key to Success & Happiness in Business & Life

By Elizabeth Duncan-Hawker

Tell Us Your Story

As a youth I felt severely disconnected from others. Through trial and error, I learned the ways to connect well with others and share my tested methodology in my book, Collecting True Friends. My father moved us seven times before high school, and with us constantly moving I had to make a decision about loneliness. What will I do to fit in? I felt lost every time we'd relocate. I had no friends. To make it even more challenging, I was a funny looking tall redhead with lots of freckles, very pale, and redheads weren't a familiar image. Today, we are called gingers. People did not understand that genetically I represented 1% of the population so instead they responded by bullying the new weird looking kid.

Like we all do in life, when your situation is not going favorably, I had a decision to make, and that's what I want you to realize today; you too have a decision on how you're going to meet a challenge. I chose not to let being bullied keep me also from being lonely in every new school. When you've had enough of your circumstance, it is up to you to decide to change your situation. That is the time to reach down inside to find your grit and courage. I decided with guts, grit, and courage to disprove that bullying taunts that nobody would like me. I watched human to human interactions so I could learn the art of - what I call - *collecting true friends*. So, how do you make yourself approachable and appealing to make friends? How do you make yourself memorable in a great way? Because we all can be memorable, but make sure to be memorable in a good way. Hmmmm... how do we show up to do that? Those constant relocations were like a computer rebooting. I realized to fit into new communities I had to learn what scientifically works connecting with strangers to convert them to friends, allies, and mentors. Fast forward to my late forties where one day I realized I felt overwhelmed and physically exhausted. I realized I'd paid a price by having a corporate career, working sixty-hour work weeks, raising three daughters, keeping a marriage together, being a good daughter, and a faithful Samaritan. I overachieved like so many women being socially compelled by thinking we are the family glue. I was financially meeting my life plan, yet emotionally I was no longer happy. I did not like my situation. So, I asked myself again, "What do I want my next decade to look like? Who do I want in my life?". I sighed realizing the people I spend the majority of my days with were not who I wanted to be spending my workdays with. Then I asked myself deeper questions. "So, where do I want to be? What types of people do I want in my life? What do I want the next five years to look like? What types of people do I want to have closer in my life"? As an executive it was a revelation to realize deadlines were no longer as important as my happiness and health. That was the day my priorities shifted. I proclaimed; I don't want to work sixty-hour work weeks anymore because I know I am worth more than this exhausting corporate career. ***My mantra became "I will seek meaningful work with nice people'.***

How did you get through this challenge?

Have you heard the term golden handcuffs? It happens when a career starts paying you so well that the creative vision of what else you could be gets blurred. Golden handcuffs incentivize you to put up with stuff not aligning to your core values. You begin to lose your way and the vibe inside of you starts feeling the misalignment. Here's the good news, that's where finding your guts, grit, and courage come in! You may not think you have grit to change your life, but you do have grit. You've been applying it to succeed this far, so listen when your internal vibe tells you to use those guts to go discover where to go next.

The guts are the part inside of you, like that middle chakra that vibrates. When you're happy about something in the future, a positive vibe feels like butterflies, but when you're unhappy, the vibe feels negative like a knot in your stomach. When I feel a knot in my stomach, I like to ask the Holy Spirit, 'where am I supposed to be?' I did that in this case and BAM! That was the moment I'd found the courage to say this is NOT where I'm supposed to be anymore. I appreciated all the blessings up to that time, but it was time to move on. To myself I repeated "One door must shut, so I can walk through another". When I have a client who feels like they can do more, I tell them it's usually because their vibes are no longer aligned with others they are near and just because you can do something really well, it doesn't mean you should keep doing it.

When I was at that pivotal moment- turning 50 - I had to be courageous to see I was capable of doing something bigger and new. So, the scariest thing besides having children was when I made that decision to resign from a huge career. I can still see the shock on my leadership's faces. They thought I'd change my mind. They even lined up my next promotion. I'll never forget the date they chose - December 8 – for the devout, this is the Immaculate Conception. As that date came closer, my vibration of discontent grew. I had that knot in my stomach (we were just talking about). I heard myself utter, 'this is not where I'm supposed to be.' I clearly realized the golden handcuffs needed to be removed. I did not need to take another promotion, I did not need to stay there, what I needed was to move on. The courage kicked in and I started my own consulting company, Red Hawk Strategic Solutions LLC on the same day I was supposed to be promoted. You can have the courage to do something new too, so believe that you've got grit - when you jump in because you sensed there is something more – it will become clearer. It may not reveal itself quickly but sit still, be quite minded, and listen more so you are open to what direction feels worth exploring. The next month after I filed my LLC company, I made myself go downtown introducing myself to an entire group of new businesspeople. I had to rebrand myself as the 'Red Hawk' and convince others to hire me. So that's courage. That was a scary thing telling strangers about my brand-new business and convincing them my experience made me credible. The crazy great thing is I was met with "congratulations on opening up your own business, well done!" That's where your connections, allies, friendships and networks built before coming in as a lifeline. Those former connections served as my backup. That's also where true friends come in to help you succeed and emotionally help you find even more courage. I called a lot of people, stood my ground, and I had the courage to see it through, because for the first couple years as an entrepreneur, your expenses generally outweigh your income. So that's the shaky part. Are you going to keep the grit and believe in yourself? Are you going to hold onto your courage and believe that your business and its profitability will truly happen? My words of wisdom are just because you can do something, and you're really good at it, doesn't mean you should continue to do it! Using grit and courage I ended a 25-year career that was keeping me back from exploring what I was capable of growing into.

What is The Gift?

My gift is showing audiences how to truly see people in front of them everyday so they can be a magnet to those worthy of their devotion. Here are a few questions I'd ask you to reflect on. Can you spot a potential true friend or business ally? As you meet people and bring them closer do you also make their life better? Or is the connection solely making your life better? Are you aware enough to practice true discernment and sense who should not stay in your circle? I ask those questions to prompt you to find your courage and grit when considering who is in your life.

Research shows that hanging with people lacking your best qualities retards your personal growth. The hard truth is that we should never meet some people for coffee. Instead, you should remain polite and respectful from a distance. Why? Because their values do not align. Meaning we should never let them get closer nor collaborate. If somebody told me when I filed to start my business on December 8, 2015, that would allow me to train thousands of professionals, help dozens of businesses increase their revenue, be on the national speaking circuit, plus write a best-selling book, I would never have believed them. All I knew was how to work for someone else. It took grit, guts, and courage and reaching a point of dissatisfaction; that was the pivotal moment for me. If I had not done that career leap, I probably wouldn't be alive today because that exhausting career literally sucked my energy, youth, and stamina out of me. I hope my story and insight helped inspire you to stand in your truth and say, "Is this where I'm supposed to be?"

What Would You Tell Somebody in Your Situation?

You're going to have to make up your mind to keep your grit when you've decided you no longer like your situation and it's time to move on. Some people are going to think you're just plain crazy when you are ready to leave their environments. Dozens of friends and colleagues called to ask, 'What are you doing?' Be able to answer the question to yourself and others, "what do you want your next ten years to look like?" and remember to include what types of people are daily in your new life.

TIP: Continue to cultivate new and keep relationships with good people today because in the future, you will need them as your backup. Make that a daily practice for your own happiness and longevity. My next advice is to honestly look at the people you've surrounded yourself with. If you've prayed on it and your intuition tells you to still do this personal growth jump forward, then you will need others of the right quality to help make it happen. If you discover instead that you are dear friends to a bunch of naysayers, regroup to collect some true friends in your life. Somebody's been your friend for twenty years, doesn't mean they're a true friend. You may have outgrown that friend or co-worker. It could be that your values no longer align. If you need help sorting out who is who in your life. My book Collecting True Friends has an easy process to guide you to create an inventory, look at your values, and look at the alignment. It allows you to create a core of people around you to tell you the truth in a way for you to get more out of life. Who are the people that are guiding you through this journey? Because you're going to need an inner circle of some very super smart people who want your best and not hold you back because they're too afraid to take their training wheels off. Psychological studies share the effects of boiled frog syndrome. If you try to take a frog and dump it in hot boiling water, the frog is going to jump out. But if you put the frog in the water and start turning up the heat gradually - which is what happens to us in the business world all the time - we stay longer than we should. If I'd stayed there much longer, I would probably not be alive. So, get the right people into your life then set your strategic plan to personally grow. My advice is to allow yourself to grow. Be open to there is more. You've been good at one thing which means another amazing talent and skill to excel at is totally possible. "Whatever you can do, or dream you can do, begin it. Boldness has genius, power and magic in it. Begin it NOW." - Goethe

By Elizabeth Duncan-Hawker, MBA

https://elizabethduncanhawker.com

https://linktr.ee/Theredhawk 1-757-477-5691

Elizabeth Duncan-Hawker, MBA, is an Award-winning Speaker and Bestseller Author who trained thousands how to connect and collaborate better and build networks. She developed her results-driven communications expertise over 20 years as an executive in an $8B company. Her clients include leaders, professionals, teams, universities, boards, associations, entrepreneurs, and nonprofits. Following Elizabeth's strategies, clients learn communication skills to hit higher goals with members, customers, employees, and communities.

She is a Certified Facilitator Trainer of the Law of Attraction. Providing workshops on how to: Build Highly effective teams, increase sales, build key relationships in business and in life, plus non-verbal techniques to attract quality business networks.

Grief is Love: Changing the Narrative

By Heidi Dunstan

Tell Us Your Story

In 2018, two days after Christmas and the day before my 40th birthday my husband passed away unexpectedly. In my process of losing him, I learned that we as a society are not taught how to grieve. To help me understand my feelings I began studying and learn more about grief and became a Certified Grief Educator. My goal wasn't the norm of helping grievers, but to teach people about grief and what to say and not say to someone who is grieving.

The reality is that we don't have a lot of education about grief. Part of the grit of life is that we live in a pain adverse culture, so grief is a topic that doesn't get talked about, it's uncomfortable. The average person will know to say 'I am sorry for your loss', send flowers or a card, attend a service, and of course we make food. That is about all we really know how to do. After that things get pretty murky, and that is when people start saying things that miss the mark.

Things like 'you're young, you'll find love again', or 'I understand grief because I went through divorce.' These people didn't say these things out of malice, or to be mean, quite the opposite, they were trying to help, but had no idea what to say and were trying their best. It takes guts and courage to speak to someone who is hurting, you can see the struggle, but it can be really hard to connect. I appreciate the courage it takes, because many grievers can also attest to the friends and family members who said nothing. So maybe they talk about other topics like sports, or the weather and avoid talking about the fact that you are hurting, or some friends may completely disappear, and that silence is deafening.

As I spent more and more time with grievers, I found out that my story was the same as many others where they have had conversations with people that were painful. We live in this world where we say or do things that just don't align, it doesn't allow someone to be seen and heard, validating their pain. In doing so, we end up minimizing how someone feels. For example, people will say things like 'at least you can get another dog,' or 'at least they're not suffering anymore', failing to acknowledge that the person right in front of you IS suffering. Sentences that start with 'At least' can make someone feel like how they feel doesn't matter. I realized that we have to do grief support differently. We've got to change the narrative around grief because all of us will grieve, and all of us will die. When I talk about grief many people around me agree that they don't know what to say, that they find these conversations to be difficult.

Grief is uncomfortable, gritty. It isn't a surprise to me that now that I work in the grief space, I have friends who say they know someone who just experienced a loss and want to refer them to talk to me.

They know their person is hurting and they don't feel equipped to support them. When in reality it is them that needs to learn and work what I call their 'grief muscle' so they can be there for their friend; they need to get the guts and courage to learn and be able to talk to their person who is hurting. Their friend can go see a grief counselor or a therapist, but they also need friends who can see them and support them exactly where they are at, and that is how I want to support them. We can't keep doing grief the same way we always have; it is not working. When I spend time and talk to people, I teach them about what grief is and that grief is love. It wouldn't hurt if they didn't love their person. When you witness deep grief, it's because you're witnessing deep love. And when you can see grief that way and see that somebody's just loving and missing their person, then what they're doing is totally normal, it changes how we approach grief and how we handle the people that are around us that are hurting.

A typical example is losing a baby. When someone says you can have another baby, it doesn't fill that void. In addition, stillborn loss and miscarriages are tricky because it's the mother and the father, and maybe the grandparents, that have that connection to the baby. Not a lot of other people have a connection or had hopes and dreams for the baby the way that you did.

Losing a baby whether it's stillborn or a miscarriage or even a child, it doesn't make sense. Parents begin to love that baby as soon as they know they are pregnant. So there is grief when they lose a child through miscarriage or a still born birth. We aren't supposed to bury babies, so the loss is significant when a child dies. It's interesting that when a child loses a parent, they are an orphan, or when a spouse loses their partner, they are a widow or widower. There is no name for a parent who's lost a child; it is such a huge loss that it can't be named.

Do you think grief gets easier?

No. I think grief gets different. I think the word 'easier' tricks people into thinking it will get better, when in fact you can still have hard days years later. Are those days as frequent as when you first lost your person? No. But when those days come, they can be just as intense, so they aren't 'easier.'

So, I like to say it changes, it gets different. I try to explain it to people this way, when you first lose someone, it can feel like you are carrying a HUGE boulder. It is so big you can't see around it and it is so heavy. As you move through the emotion's pieces break off and fall away, and your arms get stronger from carrying it. Eventually, it becomes manageable; it isn't as big and

you get used to holding on to it. Eventually it isn't that massive boulder, now it's a rock, and as it gets smaller you can carry it in your pocket. It is still there, and you still can see it, feel it, and remind you how heavy it once was. Grief and love can well up at any time (usually when you least expect it) and be heavy for a short time, but those times can be less frequent.

What are three things that people can say or do that can make it easier for a griever?

Love someone exactly where they are at. With grief we often can judge. Are you over it by now? Why haven't you emptied the closet? Grief is as individual as our fingerprint so no one will grieve the same. When you don't know what to say, say that! Say I have no words, I see how hard this is and want to be here to support you. That is better than saying nothing. You can't fix this, but you can witness it. If you say something that came out wrong, own it. Apologize, acknowledge it wasn't intentional and that you are trying. As 'Is there anything I can do to support you right now?' Rather than call me if you need me.

What would you say to someone who's going through the same thing?

Something I often say when I heard someone has had a death is 'Losing a (parent, spouse, sibling, friend, pet) is a significant loss, and my heart goes out to you. I don't need to tell them about my loss, or pain, because that may feel like I am trying to compare. A common question griever get is 'how did they die?' or 'what was the cause of death?' just like we hear on the crime shows on TV. We do have a morbid curiosity about death. Asking that question gives you information, but could make the griever relive that traumatic day, and so it isn't always helpful to ask. We need to just listen. Sometimes someone may share the story, and other times they may not, we don't need to know how someone died to support someone who is grieving. Taking the time to listen, which may mean you sit with some uncomfortable silence first. Or asking questions like 'may I ask your person's name?' or 'I would love to hear one of your favourite memories of them.' Take the time to listen, be present. You may not realize how much that helps the person who you are with.

What are you working on?

I have two books. One is a passion project. It is a collaboration book of ten of my husband's friends. We were part of our personal development group and so they've all contributed a chapter on how they knew him and how losing him impacted them. But also, the legacies he left them as a pretty special man.

I do believe it's our duty to carry on the legacies of those we've lost because that's how life continues and how we get to embrace the loss of people into the life moving forward. If we don't talk about them and we don't share, and we don't express those legacies, they can't become part of us finding the meaning of that life. The second book is about what to say and not say to someone who is grieving. It is time that we change the narrative of grief and work to be okay supporting someone who is grieving. When we approach grief knowing that grief is love it allows people to grieve with grace together.

What would you want to share with somebody that struggling with grief?

Give yourself permission to feel it. Allow the emotions to come. You do you, there is no manual on how each person grieves. Be gentle with yourself. Grief needs grace. Allow yourself to feel the pain because lots of times what I ended up doing was I asked a lot of why. Why does this hurt so much? Why am I having to do this again? Because we also think that grief is these five stages. And it's not, it's a hot mess. Seek help. I highly recommend seeing a coach or therapist who has specialized in grief. And put safe people around you either in person or online who can hold space for you when grief gets hard. Facebook has some groups for people going through different types of losses and it can be helpful to see that others are trying to work through loss, and it can help some days knowing you aren't alone.

How do you help people in this space?

Right now, I'm offering a Lean into Grief Masterclass. I'm also just starting to put together a program so that people can dive deeper into it. I am starting to build some courses to help people learn how to work their grief muscle. The words matter in grief and people are saying they wish they knew what to say so I am working to find ways to give people the opportunity. Check out my website heididunstan.ca. My Lean into Grief Masterclass runs about every six to eight weeks. They're free, and you can join a 45-minute class. It is really in those moments when you feel like you should run away, or you don't have anything to say to somebody who's grieving. Those are the moments where you're meant to lean in. Those are the moments when you're supposed to say hey, this is sticky and uncomfortable. I don't know what to say. But you're important to me and I want to be here with you. That is when we can grieve with grace together.

By Heidi Dunstan https://www.HeidiDunstan.ca

Heidi Dunstan is a Certified Grief Educator, Speaker, and International Best-Selling Author. Her passion to help others, learn more about grief, and how to support others who are grieving came after losing her husband unexpectedly in 2018. Her experience with friends and loved ones saying the wrong thing or completely disappearing gave her first-hand knowledge that many people have never learned how to grieve, which often leaves grievers to grieve in isolation. Heidi provides tips and specific things to say, and not say to help people to learn how to navigate these challenging conversations so people can grieve with grace together.

Finding Your Purpose: Navigating Fear and Regret

By Jennifer Jayde

Tell Us Your Story

The thing that took the most courage from me in my life was the first time that I really had to tap into courage. That was when I was strongly considering leaving my career in finance - a normal, acceptable career and job that I've had for 10 years - to pursue my dreams of being a photographer and traveling the world for a living. And that was terrifying to me. I know it might not sound terrifying to some people, but for me, I grew up in humble beginnings. I watched my mom struggle quite a bit and the emotional turmoil and stress and anxiety and even panic attacks that not having much money caused her when I was really young. I decided when I was very little that I wanted to be successful in life, and I would do whatever it took to make a comfortable or good living so that I could be happy. That's what I thought, that not having very much money meant that you're stressed, and you have anxiety and panic attacks and you're crying and things like that. Then I thought okay, if you hurry up and be successful, then you can be happy and you can be peaceful and relaxed.

I worked my whole life from that point on to get to some imaginary finish line where I could just suddenly kick my feet up and relax and know that I had made it in life. And I started at that moment with my lemonade stand. I also started a handmade greeting card stand and enlisted my first employee from daycare to help me make the cards. I was also really pushing to get straight A's, be the top of my class in school, and have more jobs. At one point, I was working twenty-four hours a week at the movie theater, maintaining straight A's, and playing on three different soccer teams. Anyway, it was very stressful. I put a lot of stress and pressure on myself. No one else was putting this pressure on me, and by the time I was twenty-five years old, I had my career in finance which was growing and blossoming. I had a home, I had a condo, and I had a convertible. I had my wedding at a castle, had my first baby, and I thought this was it. I thought this was the finish line. That's where I can kick my feet up and relax and say I made it, and now I can be happy. The most terrifying thing happened. I realized that after many, many years of w just constant stress and pressure on myself, I wasn't happy at all. And that was crushing because that was a lot of my life up until that point that I had put into this. I didn't know that if this doesn't make me happy, then what will? I had no idea; I was completely lost and scared that maybe I never would find happiness. If I can have all these things on paper and not be happy, then what's wrong with me and where do I go from here to truly be happy? I was feeling this kind of drifting, confused and unfulfilled, and it was terrifying for someone who feels like they should be ambitious, driven, focused, achieving, and getting to the next goal.

Around this time, someone very close to me - one of my family members, who was forty-one at the time - was diagnosed with a terminal illness, and he was given one year to live. Even on an intellectual level, I knew that life is fragile, and we could go at any time; we're not guaranteed to make it to 80, 90, or 100. I had been living my life in such a way that I had all the time in the world to figure out who I wanted to be and what I wanted to do and that if I wasted a few years unfulfilled and unhappy, well so be it. My plan was to relax when I got to retirement. I just thought, get the career going. By twenty-five, I had all those things, but then my plan from there was to just work, work, work, so that maybe I could retire at sixty instead of sixty-five. Then I can take my feet up for real and get the motor home, go on the tour, do all the things I always want to do, and see all the things I wanted to see. When my family member succumbed to their illness about eleven months later at the age of forty-two, I realized that my plan to enjoy my life in retirement had a serious flaw in the assumption that I would live to see my retirement. So that flicked on a switch in me that hasn't fully been flipped on before - in full-bodied way, not just the intellectual way - that life is meant to be enjoyed now, and that we need to enjoy whatever time we have in this moment. I remembered a dream that I had when I was growing up and that was to travel the world and take photos for a living. And I didn't do that because I didn't want to be a starving artist. In fact, I had friends and family telling me oh, don't do that, you'll be broke for the rest of your life. I kept my job in finance a little while longer, and on the evenings and weekends I was taking workshops about photography. I bought a little starter camera, and I started going to seminars and conferences, shadowing other photographers. I worked with mentors for eighteen months, doing whatever I could to practice and to learn being a photographer and starting a photography business. After eighteen months, I made the decision to walk out of that office for the very last time.

That is one of the scariest things that I have ever done because I had never practiced using my courage before, so the muscle was very weak and hadn't been built or practiced yet. It took a lot for me to walk away from that feeling of safety and security that I had clung to my whole life and step into the complete unknown and into an industry that is very saturated. Even with this massive fear, there were two quotes that helped me move forward. One was, feel the fear and do it anyway, and the second one is leap and the net shall appear. Both of these quotes told me and reminded me that there's no guarantees in life. There's no guarantees of anything other than one day this life will end. When I'm in my final hours, I want to be able to look back on my life and know that I tried doing the things I loved. My biggest fear was the fear of a life half-lived.

Many people walk around with the fear of failure. I walked around with a fear of having regret on my deathbed. Even with immense inner doubt, insecurity, unknowns, going against everything that had built up within me growing up to pursue what was in my heart. It was strong, loud voices coming to the surface. all the bells and alarms saying what are you doing? But my heart kept whispering "keep going." I'm happy to share that I hit the ground running in my photography business because I had spent those eighteen months preparing and learning from great people before me. Within a few short years I started to win awards and be published in magazines. I was being paid to travel the world and take photographs for a living. So now I tell people, facing your fear is so worth it because there is exhilaration waiting for you on the other side. It is pretty amazing that someone like me who wasn't born with any skills or talents was able to create a life that I loved and felt exhilarated by. After a few years of living my dream, I thought it would be even better to help other people to uncover and live.

How Did You Get Through This?

The best way to describe it is it felt like I had a devil whispering to me on one shoulder and an angel on the other. The devil was an inner critic, the inner bully telling me no, you can't, you're going to regret this, and all my worst fears. That little devil on the shoulder was loud and kept relentlessly putting into my mind and into my thoughts. But if I really paid attention, I could hear this little angel and it was soft, loving, and gentle, and it's very easy to miss, because the inner critic is very loud and obnoxious. It's very easy to miss but if you'll just pay attention and tune in to this little angel and listen to her encouragement. The little angel doesn't give you guarantees, promises, or exact steps, but it's just that piece of you can do this one more step. Listening to the angel on the shoulder rather than the devil would be number one. Number two is that I fast forwarded my life. I thought about it as if I was on my deathbed or in my final hours looking back, and I asked myself, would I be happier if I'd stayed in my finance job, played it safe, and didn't take any chances, or would I be happier that I gave myself a chance to see what was possible. I knew what my answer was, I needed to see what was possible for my life. I tell some of my clients that we can assume failure, or we can pursue possibility. It is always my current encouragement and practice now to pursue possibility, even when you don't have all the guarantees or all the answers because at the end of your life, you're going to be thanking yourself that you at least give yourself a chance to find out what was possible. Listening to the angel and not so much the devil doesn't mean the devil goes away. It just means that you're choosing to follow the path that is loving and encouraging and the path of possibility. If you are going to have a fear, don't let it be a failure. Let it be the fear of regret on your deathbed. And if that's the case, then you're going to try the things that scare you because there is exhilaration waiting for you on the other side. Freedom.

We regret more the things we didn't do than the things that we did. It's the things that we didn't do that will always leave us wondering what could have been. And at least if we did do it, we gave ourselves a chance.

What Would You Say to Someone in Your Situation?

Imagine there's this hike in Hawaii and you have to zigzag over a river a couple of times, but there's no bridge; you just have to do it yourself. The river has running water, and you don't know whether you might slip or fall, or what's going to happen? You could say, I can't cross this river because I can't jump that far. I can't see myself going from where I am now to where I want to be. It feels too big, too intimidating, too far, and not possible for me. Sometimes our head likes to think in extremes of black and white, so when something feels too intimidating, you've got to come back and just look for the one next step you can take. It's dipping your toe into that direction and then whatever that is, once you take that one step, then it becomes clear to see your next step. You don't have to have quit your job already because you can be doing these steps on the side, one at a time.

There's another quote: 'God does not reveal steps three and four until you have taken steps one and two.' So many people will not even attempt to cross the river because they can't see all the twelve steps to get there, and my encouragement would be don't look for all twelve steps. Look for just the first one.

How Can People Work with You?

I help people uncover and live their purpose full time. This is what brings me great joy. It is how I lived my greatest joy following the things that actually lit me up from the inside out. Now I love to help other people do the same. I do that primarily through my certification program. I have a program called 'The Awakener Certification.' I also have a free offering called the 'Find Your Purpose Challenge.' That's a free workshop that I have available. I'm guiding twenty of our Awakeners to share their inspirational yet relatable stories on how they were able to uncover and live their purpose and live a life truer to their soul rather than the one that maybe they felt they were supposed to be leading. I have all walks of life, all with different ways that people have started to live their life more authentically. It's called "Find Your Wings" and is available at jenniferjayde.com.

By Jennifer Jayde

Jennifer Jayde is an internationally, 2x bestselling and multiple award-winning Author, International Speaker, and Worldwide Alignment Coach for women that know they're meant to make a positive and meaningful impact in the lives of others. Today she uses her gifts as well as her own life experiences to inspire countless people around the world to step into their own purpose driven lives and businesses.

www.JenniferJayde.com

To access the quiz:_
https://jenniferjayde.com/FindYourPurposeQuiz

From "You can't..." to "I AM!" Defying Expectations and Embracing Purpose

By Jessy Morrison

Tell Us Your Story

I've never thought of myself as courageous, although people tell me I am. They have also called me impetuous and irresponsible, of which I am neither, I just think fast and make decisions quickly according to my gut. We really are ot encouraged in our society to follow our dreams. There is a lot of superficial chatter but not encouragement. We don't realize that it takes courage, grit and lots of guts to follow who your soul is inspired for you to become. We get so inundated trying to do everything right according to society, many people forget who they are, and come here to evolve into. As a little girl, I always played doctor and ballerina. I had been in ballet since I was four until I was 19, when I tore ligaments in both my legs. I was told that I would never dance again. So, I decided that I would go to medical school so I can help other dancers.

My guidance counselor looked at my grades and said, "No, you can't be a doctor. You are from a broken home, you are female, and you will never amount to anything. You might as well be barefoot and pregnant." I was so shocked. I didn't grow up in a culture that said you can be anything you want, but I had this dream that I knew I was meant to do somehow … maybe? (Yet it took me more than twenty years to achieve that dream). I'm the type of person you tell me I can't do something, and I will show you that I can!! First, I had to figure out how I was going to pay for medical school. I realized I also wanted to travel and see the world so what better way than to get paid to do so and save my money for tuition…or at least I thought that was my plan. You see, I spoke French, German and English, with German being my first language, so it seemed logical. I applied to every airline on the planet and started following up with every single one of them, because when I am determined I am tenacious, this girl was on a mission. I don't know what it is in me, that activates that.

I remember walking into the Royal York Hotel with my resume in hand for an airline job fair, hoping for an interview, thinking "I don't belong here". Looking around wide eyed in awe of the marble floors, crystal chandeliers, and brass handrails, I had never seen such opulence in my entire life. I was a slum kid. I was standing there, and I almost turned around, but there was a slight pressure like a hand on my back that pushed me to just go forward. I really do feel like an angel was nudging me on. "Be brave, be curious, just do it, go!"

Even when I went through my divorce and other experiences life throws at us years later, there was always something saying you're okay, just go take another step, that nudge in the center of my back. They interviewed me in French, German, and English, and within a week or so I was off to Winnipeg for training. It was so funny because looking back it happened so fast. I decided on a plan of action, took action, and poof I was there. Yet people in my past who I told, instead of congratulating me were saying nonsense "Oh, you're not pretty enough." "You don't speak enough languages." "You're only 5'7", you're not tall enough." "YOU CAN'T do this, you won't be accepted because..." Astounding, really the opinions of people, I just took it as a window to see into their minds, and their limited thinking. I'm really glad I didn't confide in a lot of people about my plans. I was raised by a single mom, and I raised my little brother - everything I did was by myself. I think they call it a trauma response, where you don't trust or rely on other people, you are overly independent. That is what was modeled to me, and it has worked well.

After three years in my dream job with Transair, I got laid off and took another job with Eastern Provincial Airlines in Nova Scotia. I found the people so friendly; nobody judged me, and everybody was welcoming. More layoffs and I wound up working in pharmaceuticals instead of going to medical school. Close to my original dream, right? This part is an example of letting the energy lead you instead of getting in your head. I fell in love, got married five months later, and people again thought I was nuts. Everybody I knew was divorced, yet our marriage lasted twenty years. For me, it was heaven on earth, except I wasn't getting pregnant and all I wanted was a family. After thirteen years, I finally maintained two pregnancies but that is also when my marriage began breaking down. Life has a way of testing you, building character and leading you on the path you were meant to be on.

I look back on that time, I was trying so hard to fit in that paradigm, but it didn't fit for me because I was blocking all the intuition. I was trying to change who I was; we learn to tone it down; we shrink to fit into the 'normal'. However, when you are in energy debt, you get sick. On our twentieth wedding anniversary my ex said he needed time to think. It took me about two weeks and lots of bill collectors suddenly phoning 24/7 to figure out he wasn't coming back, and there was no money to pay the bills. He had been my best friend for twenty years. I trusted him, but evidence was piling up that he was now somebody else. I was about to lose the house. We had one year of mortgage left to pay. I was crying in bed, but I don't think it's because I was heartbroken over him leaving. I thought I was happily married, so how come my body felt relieved? How come the whiplash I had been suffering from for six years relaxed & vanished almost overnight? Telling signs weren't they! I was crying because my dream of having a family had shifted and changed. I still love the boy that I fell in love with, I love what we had together, but if I passed him on the street right now, I wouldn't recognize him because there would be no synergy. We are no longer who we used to be, and there is no point in haunting the past, it wouldn't recognise us anyway. I was now back in a very familiar place, survival mode. I'd grown up here, learned to make decisions in this energy, and I hit a dark spot. I lacked money focused so thought the only solution for me at that point would be to commit suicide because I had this big, huge insurance policy that would leave my kids $9 million. I was crying because I didn't want to leave them - it had taken me so long to get pregnant and I was confused. My head was trying to figure stuff out, and I remember crying in bed, then suddenly the tears just stopped, and I woke up and said "No, I have to cancel the insurance policy because I cannot have this way out, this is not my backdoor! I have to be here for these kids!" My in-laws and ex weren't going to take care of them, and my mother was dying, (or at least that's what I thought at the time. BTW, she's still here, healthy and she turned 97 last May!) It hit me loud and clear though that if they went into an orphanage, they would never see the money anyway, so I had to step up, gather my grit and move forward. Did I have a long-term plan? No, I took it day by day, one step at a time, and that's what takes courage, the not knowing. But I followed my heart, I stepped out of my comfort zone, tested myself, learned new skills, and kept on going.

That was the beginning of tuning in again to my intuition, to tap into where I was being led with what to do and turning on to life and living in a new way!

With all the stress, I really did ask God for an intervention. I said "Help me, what am I supposed to be seeing that I'm not getting? What was the purpose of this? What's the bigger picture here?" I remember lamenting in my head, so sad that my kids would never know the bright young man I had married.

I apparently asked out loud but rhetorically, not expecting an answer "why did you only come now, not earlier in the marriage?" Surprisingly, the little four-year-old says, "Oh Mommy, you didn't need us then, you need us now, so we are here, now." They are my motivation, they give me courage, they give me my grit and guts!

When I look back, that answer was my freedom. It was my freedom to become me and to become the energy worker that I was meant to be. Not to be a doctor, but a healer. When I went to high school there were no healers, no job description of Energy Worker. If anything was energy related, it was the occult, or it was witchcraft, or it was looked at very negatively and laughed at.

I started diving into this world of Energy Healing because I needed to remember how to relax. Those were tough years, emotionally, financially and physically. My daughter had 'Failure to thrive', and the doctor said she wouldn't live through the year. I also had to cope with my mother's doctor telling me to make funeral preparations because my mother wasn't going to make it through the year either. My whole world was crumbling all at once. Trial by fire!

I needed to find alternatives for my daughter because Sick Kids Hospital didn't know what to do with her anymore. There were no medications we could take to help her. She had a Teflon stomach, and her food was through within an hour and a half. It's supposed to take seven to twelve to twenty-four hours for it to go through your stomach. She had no absorptive surface. She lost her hearing, her vitality, her ability to walk, to talk, to play.

That's when I started learning about celiacs disease. I went into my family history and started researching. It took another three to four years to finally get confirmation that my granola crunching ways were helping her survive and heal. Eventually I was led to Reiki. Then I discovered the energy healing that I had in my hands made a huge difference in everyone's health and vitality. The story of what I had been led to is phenomenal, mind blowing. We all live such amazing stories. (BTW my daughter is now 31 years of age, healthy and a psychic. Her path was an interesting one too). When I finally left the pharmaceutical world, my ex-father-in-law told me I was irresponsible. He said, "You cannot make a living doing energy healing. What is that? Are you insane?" "You're so impetuous," "Who do you think you are?" "What do you think you're doing? You and your children will starve and be on the street!" But no offer of help or let's make your single mother's life a little bit easier. I had been laid off three times that year from my 'steady, reliable' pharmaceutical jobs. I look back now and see it as a gift. I was right to follow my heart and intuition. At that point, I wondered how I was going to take care of my daughter, my mom, and hold down a job as well, so, I just moved my mom in with me. I figured it would be a year of hospice or palliative care. The kids and I were practicing Reiki on her every day at that point, just to make her transition comfortable and pain free. I learned EFT in 1996 when nobody was doing stuff like that, and with Reiki and EFT Mom got well. Somehow, we forgot to give my mother her prescriptions and she has been med free for twenty plus years. Doctors would ask for her list of prescriptions, and my answer would be "We give her some omega threes, vitamin D and zinc. I've also been giving her iodine drops for the last six, seven years because I heard it staves off dementia."

Personally, I have found if I take iodine and kelp, I have more energy. I don't walk around exhausted all the time. Over time we healed physically, emotionally, and spiritually. I am always amazed at how we have been conditioned to believe we can't do what we dream to do. Who are 'they' to tell me? They're not the authorities over me, I am. It is not their dream, it is mine, and it's ok if they don't encourage us to pursue our vision, they cannot see it. We have to see it, follow it, and decide "Yes!" and then do everything in our power to make that happen. And like I said, it may take years and not turn out as we expected. I don't have a backup plan, and I have always found that life has led me forward. Two years ago. I had my first $100,000 year, but my intention was never to have $100,000 a year. I was making ends meet because my dream wasn't bigger than to make ends meet.

When the coaching industry started and COVID shut down everything, that's when my business really blew up.

I was working with clients who were stuck in Holland or Dubai, or stranded somewhere in the States because they couldn't get back home, and they were referring other people to me. I was working 24/7, but I wasn't tired because what I do rejuvenates me too, but this wasn't my goal. I don't want to have $100,000 every year if I had to work this hard. I want to enjoy living my life too.

Whenever I hear a thought in my head that says, "You can't do it," I reframe that to say, "What an interesting point of view. Whose voice is that anyway? So, what about this do I need to learn so that I can move forward?" And it's not even courage, it's just knowing that we can do what we set out to do. Most people don't have a clear focus of what the next step is. If you suddenly think you can't do it, people go into that mindset and get derailed. Whereas, if you have the thought and you have the inspiration, it's yours. Take it, do it. This little head brain of ours has very little energy frequency to create. It's a storage bag, a filing cabinet, I could have looked at my filing cabinet over and over but the things that have been said to me are not my future. They were comments on what I was allowed to do, or what society lets us do, but no, I'm a creator, an Energy Healer. I didn't decide to be this, I grew into this. Life molded and crafted my skills and I brought these skills to my people.

I don't 'do business' the way it was taught either. I have in my thymus, what I imagine to be, a ball of wool. It's golden wool. It's very, very silky and soft, but it has some threads hanging off it. I cast it off in the morning before I open my eyes, and I let it go around the planet many many times. Then I start pulling it back and just locking it into my thymus and the phone will ring with the people who need my services. Yes, I know it sounds crazy, but that's how I do business. I ask God who needs me, bring them, and people come or are referred by others. When I try to do business in the masculine energy way of doing business, my business shuts down. So, I just do it my energetic way and pull-on energy. I don't have to use my head; I have to use my heart and my gut to tell me what to do. My heart and my gut have always led me, and when I do that, I don't need to gather courage; It's already there.

Words of Wisdom

I have some questions that I always ask my body and unconscious mind. Questions move energy, questions shift and create flow. Statements lock in opinions and points of view; they are not truths. The first question is, "Is that my thought?" or "whose thought was that?" I am not asking my head brain, it goes into story, I literally ask my body by placing my hand on my heart and the other hand on my belly (heart brain & Enteric brain). The body responds, it may move forward or back, it may feel expansive or collapsed, we all feel the response differently. I ask these questions for pain and disease too, because as empaths, we pick up on every body's sensation. Our body is a geiger-counter that just reads everybody's energy and frequencies. Your body says, "Notice, they have pain", but because we hear their discomfort in our head and feel it in our body, we think it's ours's. You know, when we go to the doctor and the doctor can't find anything wrong with us, it's because we're picking up other people's sensations. We are inadvertently healing others. So, the first question I always ask is "Is this mine?" The next questions are "What an interesting point of view? What else is possible? How can it get any better than this?" Then the mind stops looking for what's wrong with you and it starts looking for new possibilities and opportunities. "What else is possible?" It clears the clouds, cobwebs, dust, and the smoke, and all of a sudden you have this clear vision, and it keeps life in flow. I would say make these empowering questions your mantra and life keep getting easier.

How can People Work with You?

I work in person or on zoom, privately or in groups, people usually come to me to relieve long standing pain, like migraines, frozen shoulder. But all pain means 'Pay Attention Inwards Now', it is an imbalance of energy and often a spiritual crisis, with me they get to understand and communicate with their body, to tune it, tap in and turn on again. I'm on Tik Tok, "Energy Tuneups with Jessy." You can also look up YourbodytalkswithJessyMorrison on Instagram, and I have several groups on Facebook. Secrets of the Empowered Empath, your body talks with Jessy, Frequency healings, a Reiki group and more. I keep busy, it's my mission to have everyone tap into the beautiful energy that we are, to be healthy and happy. Drama is going to happen, but to navigate it with grace makes for a good life.

By Jessy Morrison

https://www.JessyMorrison.ca

FB link (Biz Page)

https://www.facebook.com/YourBodyTalkswithJessy

My clients call me "Their Body Whisperer" but really, I listen to the misalignment between your soul & mind using your miraculously expressive Body as your GPS to find out where communication has broken down and how to bring you back into balance again. Have your doctors said "Your tests are normal. You're fine, there's nothing wrong with you." But you know you just don't feel well, you don't feel like yourself, this isn't your normal? You are NOT fine. I help those who are experiencing pain, allergies, depression or anxiety, to reclaim their health, and feel at home in their own body, thereby creating more success in their careers and making an even bigger impact that feeds their soul.

From Isolation to Inclusivity

By Dr. Jonathan King

Tell Us Your Story

I want to tell a story about living in a very non-inclusive environment when I was growing up, and how that shaped my world and my world view about the need to have more inclusivity. I start off in my book talking about being in this perfect little world as a black boy, where all I saw were just black people. I was in a black neighborhood, and I thought that was the way we're supposed to be.

I never knew that there was a bigger world, I knew that as television. The people that I saw on that television were fictional characters, but in my mind, they were real. All the things I saw were real, but I didn't ever think I would go into that world. Then one day, my parents walked into my room and said, Jonathan, you're going to be a part of a big social experiment. I had no idea what they were talking about. And then a few days later, they took me to this all-white school system, and I was the first black kid in the town to integrate into the school. I didn't know what to expect, but it was like a roller coaster ride because all those white kids who were in my class did not want me there. And so now that

I look back on it, I realized that they were just pawns in this game. That when kids are born, they're all born with no prejudice, but by the time they were five years old, the parents didn't want this to happen. They didn't want integration. I began to get a picture of this being a non-inclusive world, and it was not what I wanted, and not what my parents wanted. My parents to me were the first inclusive leaders in my life that gave me this ambition. I also looked to my white teacher as an inclusive leader because she took a stance and said, no, we're going to treat Jonathan with respect. I'm going to help him to catch up with you because he's behind academically. After that, when things began to really move, my parents were in partnership with Dr. Martin Luther King and trying to integrate my town. We actually met him when he came to Albany. He was put in jail along with my parents, and my housekeeper didn't even let us know that my parents were in jail. It was just too much for a young mind to wrap their heads around. But in the end, going through all of that, that was the springboard to what I'm doing now. That's what motivated me to try to work on bringing about inclusivity in all aspects of my life, from not just educational environments, but work environments, and into the community I try to bring this about in the trainings that I do, and with the people that I meet where you may not like the person that you're looking at. But if we're going to live in a more united world, we have to become more open to inclusivity.

What my book is all about is that if you want to become inclusive, there are five simple steps. Now, the steps are simple, but the process is hard. The steps can be conceptualized and understood, but the process is a lifelong process. Because culture is so wide and so deep, that you can never really wrap your head around it. The approach is that you have to go in humbly. You'd have to go in with some vulnerability and if you do that, you can become experienced and knowledgeable as an inclusive leader as time goes on. This was around the time that the city wasn't locked down. My parents said Hey, enough is enough. I want my kids to have the same as white kids, so they began to protest. They got the college and high school students, and all hell broke loose. So around that time, our housekeeper was thrown in jail as well. My father, Martin Luther King and our housekeeper were in the same jail. My mother decided because the conditions were so horrible in that jail, she would take blankets and food down there. She didn't really explain to us what was going on because I was five, my sister was three, my brother was one, and she was also pregnant. When we were walking to the jail and we saw a hand coming out of the jail cell, we saw the housekeeper and we were all excited. My mother was trying to find a way to get the blankets and the food to my father, and all of a sudden, we heard this pushing, shoving, screaming, and barking to get out of the way. These two big cops were coming toward us, and we didn't know what to think. Because as a child, everything that you know about cops is about security, protection, and safety. We had no idea what was about to happen Out of nowhere, this big cop approaches my mother and says, 'you're not moving fast enough.' and shoved her to the ground. She's a pregnant woman, and all hell broke loose. As kids, we saw our mother fall to the ground and another officer kicked her in the stomach. She was unconscious; knocked out. After that, I can't remember being taken to the car. I can't remember what happened to my mom, but I was told that my mom was all scraped up and bloody, and that she got up after a few minutes, walked us to the car, and drove us back home.

When we got back home that night, what I was told was that my father actually cried because he felt like he should have been there to protect my mom. The news just began to spread, and they tried to solicit the support of the federal government, but they didn't want to get involved. Four months later, we went to the hospital because my mother was supposed to deliver the child. My father put me in the backseat, we drove to the hospital, and we waited for the birth. It felt like everything was in slow motion. When my mom came to the glass door, they brought her out in a wheelchair and, like a hawk, I was just looking for the baby, because I was so excited about this little new sibling that was going to be my little brother. They brought her down to the car, opened the door, and gently picked her up out of the wheelchair, put her in the car ,and shut the door.

Little Jonathan said, 'Mommy, where's the baby?' And I just kept asking that question. She never turned around. She never said anything about the baby. My father never said anything about the baby. And we get to the house. Nothing was said about the baby ever. We never talked about the death, and I think it was so traumatic for my mom and dad that they could never talk about it. Years later, when I had to give a talk about civil rights history in the making, my mind went back to them. When I finally realized that the incident really did happen, I was just blown away. A few days later, Dr. Martin Luther King gave a press conference in our backyard to talk about what had happened and the sacrifice that my mother had made. He did something that was interesting, because when my mother was beat up that day and the word got back to Albany, the blacks started rioting in the city. It was a big embarrassment for Dr. King, because he supported a non-violent stance. So that particular day, he said, 'We need to have a day of penance for what happened, because this is supposed to be a nonviolent community, we're not supposed to react.' For the next two or three days, Dr. King, my father, and others went throughout the community, and talked about the importance of non-violence in the city.

I don't have any hate toward those policemen because it really was not their fault to a certain degree because they were menaced by their own prejudices. When you're brainwashed at a very young age like that, it's almost like what happened to Germany all over again. That's why all those negative things in Germany happened, because people believed so strongly in what they were taught, and they had no way of getting out of that. So that's why I'm always thinking, what if we can get to the children and prevent them from having that kind of implicit bias towards other people of different races and ethnicities?

How Did You Get Through It All?

Part of it was just having a deeper understanding about human nature. Being able to travel and see how implicit bias works. Living in Japan, one of the highlights of my life is to see that all of these people in Japan and in Asia, they think a certain way because of the way they're taught, but it doesn't mean that people are stuck in their thinking. It just means that the younger you are and the longer you embrace those thoughts, the harder it's going to be to get out of this implicit bias. I've just been able to take a spiritual attitude toward people in general, knowing that people are innocent.

The gift for me was understanding that there are choices that people can make. People can hold on to their anger about something, or they can look at the bigger picture and say, 'What can I do to get out of this?' Dr. King, for example, was a person I looked up to, he went through a lot of challenges. He suffered the ultimate sacrifice when he had to give up his life. But I look at it like we are all able to be change agents. And I'm standing on the shoulders of my parents. I'm standing on the shoulders of people like Dr. King, and my gift, I would say, is insight to try to bring about unity among different backgrounds.

I've been working in all these different organizations from the time I was eighteen years old, and most times I'm the only one of color. I've been able to see all the different ways that people have tried to sometimes keep diverse populations marginalized in those particular work environments. What I try to do now is make people aware of how to be more inclusive, because most people refrain from doing that. They want to take the easy way out, and the easy way out is just associating with the people that you look like and the people with which you have some kind of cultural affinity with. After going through all the different elements, I put together a program and this program is aimed at helping people to acknowledge that they have implicit bias, and that's very difficult for some people, because they don't want to admit it, and they don't want to be exposed, and I think it's a bad thing. The second thing is how do you diffuse your bias? How do you confront the bias? Looking at this five-step plan, the next thing - once you diffuse the bias - is being able to align yourself with people that look different from you. And that's another hard step to consciously align yourself. What I mean is, what are we going to do to get to know that culture better because people just associate with others who look like them? I put together the five steps on how that's done as follows:

A stands for acknowledge.

D stands for Disrupt

A stand for align

P is participating

T is to take down and tackle any form of systemic racism

I think the critical piece right here is that if you take something like implicit bias assessment, it can home in on what those issues might be. But the key here is understanding that everyone has it. There is no one free from this in particular. I don't want to call it a problem, but it is something that's attached to how we're raised. Everybody is clued in with it.

Words of Wisdom

I would say, don't be hard on yourself when it comes to try to be inclusive, and don't look at yourself as having to be perfect. Know that this is a marathon, it's not a sprint. It could take some people years; it could take a year for somebody and six months for another. The first step is just realizing and acknowledging that you have implicit bias. This exercise is not only for whites. Some people think it's whites who need this, but everybody needs it. And I give the example of my wife, who is from Kenya. She told me that in her country, there are 30 different tribes. I asked her how they thought about each other, and she said, 'we all hate each other.'

How Can People Get in Touch with You?

They can go to my website, which is JKingconsulting.com, where they can find out more about what I do. They can find out more about the book and what's in the book, and then if they want services, they can reach out to me through that website.

By Dr. Jonathan King

https://www.JKingConsulting.com

Dr. Jonathan King is a DEI (Diversity, Equity, & Inclusion) Consultant who works closely with Colleges and Universities to facilitate their journey toward becoming more inclusive at every level of the organization. His mission is to create workplaces that champion the idea of creating unity in diversity, where all employees are respected and valued regardless of their color, ethnic heritage, nationality, religion, gender, or sexual orientation.

Zone of Potential: Making the Most of Your Opportunities

by Karin Schultz

Tell Us Your Story

I contemplated various stories I could share, and one that stood out as a significant turning point in my life came to mind. It started during my year in brick-and-mortar college, when I found myself caught up in a whirlwind of parties, reckless spending, and neglecting my studies. Eventually, I reached a breaking point where not only was I struggling academically, but I also made the tough decision to drop out of college altogether. Realizing that I couldn't continue squandering money without anything substantial to show for it, I made a pivotal move to Arkansas for a period of time. During my time in Arkansas, I found employment at a hardware store, and while it was a decent job, I couldn't shake the feeling that it wasn't my true calling. This inner struggle led to a period of deep depression as I questioned the direction of my life.

Faced with a failing car and financial hardship, I realized I needed to make a change. In a moment of decision, I reached out to an old boyfriend who promptly came to pick me up and brought me back home. Upon returning home, my father presented his terms to all his children: either attend school full-time while contributing by buying groceries or pay room and board if we chose to stay at home. I opted to give the room and board arrangement a try, willing to explore this new path. I returned to my previous job, hoping for a second chance, but they informed me that I had effectively resigned when I left. A wave of uncertainty washed over me, as I realized I lacked the structure and discipline I needed, especially as a college student. Simultaneously, the pressing need for employment weighed heavily on me, and I knew I couldn't stay in that situation any longer. On November 9, my father and I walked into the recruiting station, and I approached the Air Force recruiter, expressing my interest in joining. As I began filling out the paperwork, a burning question nagged at me. Despite the recruiter's insistence that I refrain from asking questions and focus on the paperwork, I reached an impasse. I couldn't proceed without answers. So, once more, I asked my question. He was very rude and refused to answer my questions unless I was finished with my paperwork. I wasn't. Without hesitation, I tore up the paperwork and discarded it in the trash, turning to my father and saying, "Come on, Dad, let's explore the Marine Corps option."

I approached the Marine Corps recruiting office and promptly enlisted. The recruiter asked, "When would you like to depart?" My immediate response was, "As soon as possible." However, the prospect of leaving so soon, given my state of depression and the weight I had gained (which didn't align with Marine Corps standards), made me reconsider. I realized I needed to shed some pounds, get physically fit, and prepare myself for the demands of Marine Corps life. My knowledge of the Marine Corps was limited to what my father had experienced, and I had no idea what to expect in terms of the challenges and experiences that lay ahead. In January of 1985, I enlisted in the Marine Corps and embarked on a journey that was quite unfamiliar to me. I had to start from scratch, learning everything from the ground up during boot camp because I had very little prior knowledge of military procedures and protocols. Surprisingly, despite my initial lack of familiarity, I managed to excel and found myself in the honor platoon when I eventually graduated.

What Were Some of the Challenges?

When it came to making a decision about joining the military, I realized that I possessed just enough knowledge to make an informed choice. A few years earlier, my father had advised me to pursue a college degree, and I had wholeheartedly agreed, vowing never to consider joining the military. However, life had other plans, and I learned never to say 'never' again. During the two months between November and December, I dedicated myself to getting into physical shape, preparing for what lay ahead. Upon entering boot camp, I found myself surrounded by other recruits, most of whom were already well-versed in military practices. They knew how to march, how to stand at attention, and had prior exposure to military drills. In contrast, I was starting from scratch, which presented a significant challenge. Throughout this journey, I relied heavily on my determination and unwavering resolve to persevere, even when faced with the daunting task of catching up to my peers who were more well-versed in military procedures.

How Did You Get Through This?

First and foremost, it's crucial not to engage in constant comparisons with others since everyone's journey is unique. Second, humor plays a vital role; learning to laugh at oneself is essential, especially when we make inevitable mistakes or find ourselves in unfamiliar territory. It's a reminder that none of us can know everything or excel at everything, and rather than becoming frustrated, it's better to embrace the moments with humor. Frustration is a part of life, and when it does creep in, taking a step back to chuckle can be incredibly relieving. Embracing structure has its merits, but it's equally important to allow for flexibility, recognizing that everyone's approach to discipline differs based on their individual lives and circumstances. Ultimately, finding enjoyment and fulfillment in the work before you are key to a fulfilling journey.

The Marine Corps, while offering numerous advantages, also presents its fair share of challenges that demand continuous self-validation. As a woman navigating this predominantly male environment, I often felt the need to prove my worth as a Marine at each duty station. However, this didn't mean I had to become a chameleon; I could still remain true to myself while upholding the honor and respect expected in the profession I had chosen. If ever discontented, the option to move on and exit the situation was always available. Despite the obstacles, I cherished the mutual exchange between the Marine Corps and myself—the growth and contributions I received and gave back to this elite institution.

What Would You Say to Someone in Your Situation?

View every direction you choose as an opportunity for learning and growth. Trust your instincts; if a path doesn't align with your true calling, you'll sense it. Moreover, don't hesitate to explore alternative avenues or entertain the idea of moving on. There's no need to fear change or admit when you've reached a point where it's time to part ways. Recognize that the journey you've had has been mutually beneficial, but there's a vast world of possibilities awaiting you, and making room for new experiences can be immensely rewarding for both you and the path you leave behind. It's also essential to ensure you're well-prepared with knowledge before embarking on a new journey. In my book, 'Zone of Potential,' I delve into this concept extensively. Reflect on what you're willing to commit to and what's non-negotiable, identify your strengths and the activities that deplete your energy. Assess whether your support structure genuinely encourages your aspirations, as it's vital to be in an environment where you feel valued and welcomed. Additionally, remember to cultivate resilience, persevering through challenges, and finding contentment in your current circumstances. Always keep in mind that you can pivot and change your path whenever you feel the need.

Once you've made that decision, it's incredibly liberating. The constant back-and-forth of "Should I stay, or should I go? Should

I, do it?" can weigh heavily, leading to stress and anxiety. However, once you make a choice and embrace the understanding that there will be valuable lessons at every turn, you can shed the burden of uncertainty and fully commit to your chosen path, lightening the load on your shoulders.

What is the Gift?

The incredible gift of joining the Marine Corps was the realization that I had become part of something far greater and more meaningful than just myself—an experience that had a profound impact not only on my personal life but also on a global scale. This sense of purpose and significance was immensely satisfying, and it also motivated me to maintain physical fitness and truly prioritize my overall well-being. The second gift of my Marine Corps journey was the development of courage. Being a Marine instilled in me a deep sense of leadership right from the start, and these leadership skills proved to be highly transferable. After retiring from the government, I carried this newfound courage and leadership experience with me into my current work as an executive and leadership coach. This transition marked a pivotal moment of self-awareness, where I recognized my need for structure, discipline, and the pursuit of meaningful work, exemplified in the creation of my book, 'Zone of Potential.' It's a testament to the idea that we all navigate our personal zones of potential, and it's up to each one of us what we do in that space. My gift lies in capturing the wealth of lessons and experiences I've garnered and presenting them to the world through my book.

How Can People Work and Get in Touch with You?

You can find me on my website, Zoneofpotential.com, where every page offers an opportunity to connect with me. I'm also active on various social media platforms such as Facebook, Instagram, and LinkedIn, providing multiple avenues for reaching out. When you do connect with me, you'll have the opportunity for a 30-minute inquiry call. This call serves as a chance to not only determine if my services align with your needs but also to gauge if we're a good match because our energies and goals may vary. I may or may not be the right fit for your specific requirements, or you may be seeking something different from my perspective, in which case, I can offer guidance or connect you with the right resources. As the 2023 President of the International Coaching Federation for the state of Maryland, I have access to a network of fellow coaches whom I can introduce you to if needed.

By Karin Schultz

https://www.ZoneOfPotential.com

https://www.linkedin.com/in/karin-schultz-570916152

Karin Schultz is founder of "Zone of Potential," a company offering Executive and Leadership Coaching. With four decades of expertise from the US Marine Corps and Government Service, she empowers and encourages clients to achieve their greatest success. A dynamic athlete, #1 Int'l Best-Selling Author, and community champion, Karin brings passion, power, and purpose to every endeavor.

Beyond the End of the Road: From Speaking Event to a Coma in Less Than 48 Hours

By Ken Course

Tell Us Your Story

My story starts during my life as a road warrior.

I was a speaker, trainer, and event manager working for multiple major speaking companies, which meant long periods of my life where I was on the road doing events. Many months this meant fifteen to twenty days a month where I'd be flying and traveling all over the world.

As you can imagine, that causes a lot of challenges and strain on a personal life and relationships. My team and I are in the middle of one of the biggest campaigns I ever worked on - the launch of the third New York Times best-selling book that I worked on - with more work and stress than most could imagine. The culmination of these efforts was a giant multi-speaker event which had industry legends such as Les Brown and Mark Victor Hansen. The team had worked so hard for over a year to get to this point to reach the event with enough drama to fill an entire book on its own. Upon getting home from that event I felt sick - it's common to come down with some "event crud" or the flu. No worries, I'm laying in bed, taking my medicine, and relaxing.

But within a few hours, I realized that something felt very different. I'm quickly feeling sicker than I have ever been in my life. I have a horrible fever, shaking, hot and cold spells, and I can't keep down any food or drink. The experience felt a lot like what COVID means to most people now. After a few hours, I rolled over to my girlfriend at the time and I said that I think I need to go to the emergency room. They run every test imaginable, but everything comes back negative. Okay, it's normal, probably just some sort of bad virus or infection and I'll go home with some antibiotics.

After returning home, things degraded quickly. Within eight hours, I'm so much worse. At around six or seven in the morning, I am looking at myself in the mirror thinking, *"I've never looked like this in my life; I look like death."*

Back to the emergency, and this time they ordered more intense scans and tests. The tests reveal that I have severe pneumonia in both of my lungs, reducing my breathing capacity by *over 50%.* I was immediately admitted to the hospital and put in the ICU. My memory starts getting very fuzzy and hazy here, but I distinctly remember both the nurses and doctors worrying that I wasn't going to make it. My last memory is hitting the call button gasping for breath before the world fades to black. I'm in a coma for 10 days. I lost most of my body fat and muscle strength. My father - who was still alive at the time - flew out for support. My sister was there along with a lot of people from work, but it really wasn't looking good. During this time, by sheer luck, one of the nurses had a minor accident with inserting a feeding tube. As a result, they did an ultrasound which revealed that there was an issue with my liver. As soon as they discovered that problem, they changed the treatment, and I started to recover almost miraculously.

When I woke up, I was still on life support and intubated. I had no idea where I was or what had happened. So, when you're in ICU, there's a nurse that changes the date on the board to notify the team when you were last checked. When I first woke up and saw the date, my first words were mentioning that the date was wrong. I had no awareness of the time that had passed, it just felt like snapping my fingers and 10 minutes had passed. However, when people started talking to me after I was conscious, they would mention things they'd said or done while I was out, and I would have clear memories of their visit. I knew I was hearing and receiving information and I knew that people were there. My dad wasn't in the room when I woke up initially, but somehow, I knew my dad was there. From my experience, people in comas are hearing you, its processing, but it feels like a strange dream.

While all this was going on and I was being intubated, one of my vocal cords was nicked and damaged. This means that when I was recovering, I was unable to speak. As a speaker, coach, and trainer, my voice is my living. Not to mention that I'm also a singer and musician. Doctors couldn't say when I would be able to talk, and this long painful process went on for almost two years. All of this resulted in a PTSD diagnosis. The whole time I'm going through this, I'm also having horrible flashbacks and attacks. This experience was a true identity crisis, because I am known as a loud rambunctious kind of guy, and I had no idea what I was going to be or what I was going to do in the future. There was no certainty that my voice was ever going to come back, and I went through a lot of punishment to make sure it did. I would go to a specialist every week who would perform a nasal scope to look at my vocal cords. This meant that once a week, for months, the doctor would run a tube up through my nose and down the back of my throat with a camera. This went on for months so that the doctor could look at my vocal cords and see if I was responding to the treatment.

I was especially insistent *because I needed my voice.* I spent the entire time in treatment trying to get back to work as quickly as I could despite symptoms and problems that persisted for over two years. All that said, I will still always remember when I finally started responding to treatments and got the good news that surgery wasn't required. If I had needed the surgery, it would have been very likely that I would never have my voice back as it had been before. I'll always remember the first time I was able to sing again, at a karaoke party that wasn't recommended by my doctor. It's still one of the happiest moments of my life to go through all of those challenges and realize that I would indeed be able to sing and speak again. This experience is something that has defined and shifted my perspective on literally everything: my relationships, my career, how I worked with people, and my own priorities for the future. It led me down a path to start working on myself personally, obviously because I needed to work on the PTSD, but also in realizing how I wanted to connect with people.

What do I want my legacy to be once everything is all said and done?

In the end, doctors never figured out exactly what happened to me. I was 29 when this started, and this isn't typical for someone of that age. All of a sudden, here I am meeting my own mortality and realizing that I'd better make some decisions about who I want to be and what I want my life to be going forward. I've kept all the reminders from that time in my life because it forced me to grow up and be more grateful for what I have - especially my voice and music. It's something that is deeply reflected when I work with people now. I think about it all the time and how I want people to experience me as both a person, a friend, a colleague, and a speaker because I know that my time isn't forever. I want to make sure that I have the impact I want to have. I want people to think of me and think positive things whenever possible, though I can't please everyone. Nobody's perfect, but that's always my intent - to make sure that I'm really serving people as honestly as possible.

How Did You Get Through This?

The biggest change was actively engaging in positive self-reflection, because obviously with post-traumatic stress disorder, your brain is sabotaging you in many ways which are uncontrollable. My brain had to be refocused to focus me outside of these catastrophic experiences and thoughts. I was fortunate to have met a great trainer at the time who supported me in this journey. She described that when you look at a brain scan of a person with PTSD, it appears as “valleys and dark spots” in the brain. People with extensive PTSD have many more of these “dark spots,” with more and more being discovered about brain health with emerging research in neuroscience. To avoid those breakdowns, I had to develop new pathways and new ways of thinking that kept me from going into those valleys because once I was stuck there, I couldn’t get out. It’s the entire nature of the disorder.

I had to develop this whole new way of living and understanding gratitude, peace, and facing the positive of what was happening in my life. This didn’t come naturally to me at all as I’m more of a cynic or skeptic at heart. I'm certainly not perfect. I make a lot of mistakes. I didn’t take many of those practices very seriously. I'd hear about “having a spiritual practice” or “gratitude” and all those “Kumbaya” things, but I was too busy. This experience was really a wake-up call to say no, these are serious things that I and many others need in their life, especially during times as dark as that time became for me. I wouldn't be able to do what I do and work with people the way that I do if I didn't start to become more self-aware. Understanding basic practices like journaling, gratitude, and meditation - which I still struggle with doing regularly - are just forms of positive self-reflection. Where am I right now? How am I feeling about what's going on in my world? Do I need to speed up? Do I need to slow down and take better care of myself? I'm a workaholic, like many entrepreneurs, so I needed to become aware of those tendencies and develop a stronger inner and outer support network.

What is the Gift?

You don’t know what you’ve got ‘til it’s gone. You’ve got to value yourself and what you have. That might feel like an “after school special message,” but it's true. Personally, I didn't realize what I had in my voice and how powerful it was until I didn't have it for a long time. It’s such a core part of my identity. Realizing how important that one aspect of myself is and putting value on it was critical for me. Simple practices can prevent major crises from happening. The gratitude practices, the journaling, taking time to relax, and focusing on your breathing. A great exercise I learned during this time was focusing and staying very present while eating a meal. A lot of people wolf down food when eating and aren't grateful for the experience. These little things become the building blocks to your day.

Even just taking a deep breath into your diaphragm - you can't help but calm down. When you relax your body, your emotions will often relax as well.

How Can People Get in Touch with You?

I specialize in helping people who make money with their experience, expertise, story, and content. Whether you're a creator, speaker, trainer, author, or an expert of any kind - we serve you. My business, Now Presenting You, puts you front and center during a wide variety of workshops, training, and coaching programs. If you're in the process of finding your voice or creating a content-based business, find me at nowpresentingyou.com.

By Ken Course

https://www.NowPresentingYou.com

Trusting Your Gut and Finding Your Zone of Genius

By Kimberly Crowe

Tell Us Your Story

I'm proud to be a speaker in the transformation space. I show entrepreneurs, coaches and healers how to grow their business by getting speaking opportunities in front of their ideal audience. I am proud to be an award-winning, international inspirational public speaker, keynote speaker, TEDx speaker, and an authority on speak-to-sell. I've worked with Kelly Falardeau to become a five-time best-selling author. I have a weekly online show, Speakers Playhouse which is a gamified networking show to connect show hosts with expert guests. My mission is to make speaking on stages super accessible and super fun for entrepreneurs, coaches and healers to share their message in the world. That's all wonderful now, but it hasn't always been this way. I, like many of our readers, went to college, graduated, and got myself a "good, stable corporate job" with health insurance and a 401K. I joined a fortune 1000 company, and I diligently set about working my way up the company ladder. I did well and I became a leader, rose through the ranks, and eventually became an executive director.

But as I got to the top of the ladder and I peeked behind the curtain, it wasn't what I expected at all. Many of the executives at my level and above seemed truly unhappy. To me, they seemed bitter, old, angry, frustrated and unfulfilled. I thought to myself - gosh, after seventeen years of climbing, this is not even a ladder I want to be on. And that was a moment of profound realization. Even though I was making very good money, I had found myself in what they call "golden handcuffs." I had risen to a point at a company where I was getting paid so well, it didn't make financial sense to quit, but I didn't love the work anymore, I wasn't having any fun - and it was no longer fulfilling. It was working for a paycheck - and a very nice one - but it was not something that I wanted to do anymore. I wanted to quit. However, my husband, at the time, was not really excited about me leaving a job that was paying so well and was not supportive of me quitting, but I was very very unhappy. It was.

miserable, getting up and going to work. I hit a crisis point. What helped me turn the corner was my son. One afternoon, my son met me at my front door, and he said "Mom, I have a problem. I'm fifteen and a half and we're going into summer. And fifteen and a half is exactly the wrong age. I'm too young to get a summer job, and I'm too old to go back to summer camp,"

I thought to myself… How great to have someone else's problem to focus on for a little while! While I was focusing on my problem, I was struggling. I couldn't seem to do anything right. As women, I think sometimes we're really good at helping other people and not so much helping ourselves. I was delighted to distract myself with my son's quandary. I said, "You know what? You're never too young or too old to be an entrepreneur. So why don't you and I create a business around what you just love doing, just something that you think would be fun." We set about creating a business around what he was naturally good at, and what he loved to do. He was really good at acting, he was funny, he enjoyed getting on stage, he enjoyed reading books to kids in the local library, and he enjoyed doing improvisation on stage. We put all these cool things that he was good at into Google and up came the idea: Why don't you be an audiobook narrator? His eyes lit up and he asked: "Can we get paid for that?" I knew we were onto something! We went to Amazon and bought a whole bunch of stuff to do audiobook narration and we started this business. We were super excited about it, and I remember thinking… Gosh, this is how it should feel. This is how life and business and fun and family should feel. It shouldn't be slogging through the frustration and straining to be able to just make a buck. It should be fun. I made a decision that from that point on, I would never do something just because it paid well. Or even just if I was good at it. My motto became: "If it's not fun, it's not worth doing." From there, I started to follow that motto and started to recite that dream every time I'd run into a snag or a struggle. I'd ask, 'Is this fun? And if it's not fun, why am I doing it? Just set it down and go find something else.' Now, it's not that you stop doing everything. It's not that you sit on the couch, and you lay around and you wait for the world to come to you. It's that you start doing the things that you enjoy doing.

As you step into that, you light up with this internal energy and start to glow, and people start to be attracted to you. Other people come to you and want to know how you do it. And from there, you can start helping other people with that service. Because what is inside you that lights you up is different from anything that anybody else does. And you're going to do it with your own special version of magic.

What Would You Say to Someone Facing Your Situation?

I would say trust your gut. Go in and figure out what you love about what you're doing right now and do more of it. And figure out what you don't love about what you're doing right now and do less of it. I think that that's really something that we don't really believe is possible. We believe that the struggle has to be hard. We believe that hard work is what people pay money for. We believe that you've got to struggle to earn. We believe that money doesn't grow on trees. We believe that you've got to really work hard doing the things you don't want to do to get the paycheck, and I'm here to tell you I'm living proof that that is not true. It's just that's not where I am, but where I am is magic for me, and when you show up in your magic, you attract people and you become glowing. That glow attracts your ideal audience, and there are people who come to you because of who you're showing up as. A lot of us try to emulate other people. Maybe they bring you into corporate and they say: this is how we do things here. Do it this way. And maybe you get a chance to add your own little secret sauce to it and it's going to be your own little magic. Some will thrive doing that, but some will waste away. If you're feeling like you're wasting away and what you do no longer matches with who you are, consider that that's probably not what you're brought here to this planet to do. Life is supposed to be fun! If you're not having fun, it's an indicator that you're off the path where you can contribute the most. There's magic inside you and if you're hiding it, doing somebody else's dream, you're working to help somebody else create their dream. Trust in the idea that, if you don't like doing something that's a red flag - for you. There are people in the world who probably love doing what you hate doing. There are people who are really looking forward to having a job doing exactly what you hate doing. Because that's what they think is fun, and that's what they're meant to do. If you're feeling stuck and frustrated, listen to that little voice and don't let anybody in your life talk you out of it. If you know that you're meant to do something else, check it out, pursue it. Trust your gut. I'm not saying you have to quit your job immediately. But start exploring other possibilities, even in your current company. As an employee, take a few minutes to tell your boss what you want to do. As an employer, ask your employees what they want to do more of.

What is the Gift?

What you are feeling inside - what your gut is telling you - is correct, and you need to trust it. If you're feeling awful or frustrated or angry, it is an indication from the universe that your off track. That you're not in your zone of genius, and you're not in the place that you're the best contribution to the world. If you're frustrated, angry or bitter, you are probably in the wrong place, and maybe working someone else's dream. If you're feeling like something's off, it probably is. When you feel something light you up, explore it! Go out of your way to seek more of it out. The gift in it for me was that I got a chance to walk away from something that was making me very unhappy into something that gives me joy every single day.

How Can People Get in Touch With You?

My favorite way to connect is to have you come to our free event which happens every single Thursday. It's a show called ***Speaker's Playhouse***. You can find it at https://www.speakersplayhouse.com. It happens every Thursday from 10:30 am to noon Pacific. It's a live interactive show where experts can find speaking opportunities and show hosts can find guests. It is a networking event that is fast paced, fun, joyous, energetic, and you're going to have the best 90 minutes of your week. See you there!

By Kimberly Crowe

https://www.SpeakersPlayhouse.com

From Adversity to Empowerment

By Laban Ditchburn

What's Your Story of Grit, Guts and Courage?

When you asked me this question, I was putting some deep thought into the way that I can best serve people; that's my philosophy. How can I add value to people's lives? It doesn't matter who they are. Based on a lot of feedback that I've gotten from people rather than my own thoughts is probably the best direction, and what it is for is that this August 26, 2023, is my seventh year of sobriety from alcohol. It's been even longer for drugs, gambling, philandering, limiting beliefs, and negative self-talk. My journey really started out as a three-and-a-half-year-old when mum and dad split up; nothing more innocuous than that, but I know people will identify with the story because 50% of all marriages that end in divorce. The challenge with that was the kids - my brothers and I - were used as pawns in custody battles, and with parents trying to get back and forth at each other. There were trips to foster homes, being stolen away, intervention orders, and all kinds of crazy stuff that no child really is going to benefit from experiencing.

What I came to learn - after hitting rock bottom in 2015 - was that a lot of the drama that I was bringing into my life was a direct result of me operating from a place of victim mindset; the whole "Woe is me." It wasn't until I started looking at what positive attributes, I got from my parents that my mindset started to shift and that whole process allowed me to start this healing process. I had no objection for people going through 12 step programs or whatever they need to use to become successful in their own healing journey. For me, I didn't need it, because I was able to get to a point where I was able to address the reason for wanting to escape. When I started looking at the reason why I wanted to escape, all I needed to do was adjust those behaviors, ditch and unlearn a lot of the dysfunctional stuff, and then relearn the functional stuff.

I did that through asking for help, and there's a wonderful quote from Les Brown. He says, "Ask for help not so that you appear weak, but so that you can remain strong. Keep asking for help until you get it." That was in 2015 back in Australia, when I reached out to the gambler's helpline. I was a prolific, functioning gambler and I used it to escape the tyranny of my life. As I started to become more and more conscious and empower myself with knowledge, books, podcasts, and conversations with people that were further along than I, I realized that not only did those experiences no longer have power over me, but they were actually my new fuel source, and I can use those as powerful anecdotes to be able to inspire and help other people. I think that's the message that I really want to get across to people today; whatever part of the journey that you're on from healing from the abuse, drugs, violence, or whatever it might be, you will realize that there might be more to life than the nine to five that you're doing. I've been given this beautiful responsibility to share this message of hope, inspiration, and empowerment to the rest of the world, and to do that to the best of my ability. Can I change the world as a single entity? Absolutely not. We need more and more people to do what they're doing, and to understand that your impact can have a ripple effect that can go on to completely transform entire generations of people. When the 'Why' becomes clear, the 'How' becomes easy. You don't need to know how to do it, you just need to know why you're doing it.

How Did You Get Through It?

It's a question I get asked a lot and it's the same answer for everyone because it's the truth. I was in horrendous amounts of emotional, spiritual, and physical pain, and the thought of continuing on my current journey was far worse than whatever road I had to take to get the work done, and I think that's one of the things that people might miss.

At times we try to save people that don't want to be saved, and that's one of the more damaging things we could do. It's very well intended, but it doesn't serve the person who's trying to be saved at all, it ends up pushing them away. In many cases, the most effective strategy is to lead by example, so that was a stiff lesson for me. I remember in 2020, when I started my podcast, I came up with this great name; it's called "Become Your Own Superhero" podcast. I started interviewing these incredible people. My father had gone through major health challenges, so I deliberately started interviewing doctors and medical experts that I knew could help my father. In these interviews, I would ask them questions that related exactly to my father's own health situation, then I would finish these incredible recordings with priceless information and send it to my dad. He never listened. He never wanted help. He was content living his life. It was up to me to accept him and love him for that. Did I need to spend every waking day with the guy? No, I didn't. Did it push our relationship apart compared to what it was like beforehand? Absolutely it did. But that was a necessary sacrifice in terms of me setting that clear boundary, and because I was able to do that, it created space in other areas of my life to allow other high quality human beings in there that did want help. I will always love my father, and I'm unbelievably grateful for the wonderful gifts that I took on from his genes. What I got from him when he was in my life and could be in my life, that's okay. It's okay now, that's what's been so liberating. There's no need to drink the poison and try and hurt someone else.

What Would You Say to Someone Going Through the Same Thing?

Have you ever hated someone that you've never met before? Or from afar? So then is it not possible that we can love people without having met them as well? Absolutely. I would say to this person that I love you. I love you. I would also say to treat yourself like someone you really care about, understanding that no matter what you've done, once you recapture, reclaim, and take full ownership of it, that's when you will become unbelievably empowered. That's how I wrote my book. I put everything out there that I had done - not from a place of victimhood - from a place of ownership. I also keep saying it holds no dominion over me. It took a little bit of time to get to that point, but it's one of those things that you don't need to suffer with. There's a very famous quote from Seneca, one of the stoics, that says," It's always worse in our imagination than it is in our head." I'm paraphrasing that statement, but you get the gist. It always does, and counting the truth is a very cathartic and liberating experience. When you operate from a place of integrity, that energy is picked up by other people that operate like that, too. You tend to polarize away a lot of the negativity in your life organically, and start attracting more high quality, integral in alignment, and purpose- driven people. Anna and I's life has just evolved into what I call a daily miracle. I got interviewed on a really big show yesterday - which is a career highlight for me – with an audience of millions or billions. In conversations with the guy, he says, "Hey, I'm going to Dallas on the second - taking the jet. Do you want to come along?"

This is what I imagined, laughing about the material things, but it's not even about that. It's about the connections, engagements, and opportunities that become presented to us. I think people get confused when they are indoctrinated at school and college about what actually fulfills us. When you get a good job, and you get the family and stuff, its actually fulfillment, which is the thing that people are actually looking for. The material stuff will always be an unlimited byproduct of the value you're creating in the world at scale. There are so many incredibly wealthy people who are absolutely miserable because they're not fulfilled. I think

I have a very deep connection to Source. I'm not a religious guy in any capacity, but I'm very, very spiritual, because I've witnessed the miracles that are created from that connection to Source for years now. It's beyond any shadow of any doubt. It's beyond mathematical improbability, that it's an accident, and that's one of the most liberating things; knowing that I have this army of angels that are looking after me. It's titillating and exciting, the prospect of being on a private jet, but it's like having a comfy bed and hot running water every day; you become acclimatized to it. It's only when you visit a third world country that doesn't have that; it's the experience. It's the time with the person on the plane that people pay six figures to spend an afternoon with, and we get it for nothing. From a monetary point of view, it's not nothing, because the person inviting us on will be on the receiving end of service, because that's just the discipline that's been ingrained and indoctrinated into my own thinking. It's the most effective pathway to progress forward in life and to be resilient to all the challenges that come to you. People need to go through their own experience to come to these realizations, and hopefully they get to them faster than I did. But you're exactly where you need to be right now. You would have heard this statement before.

I do believe that we are infinite spiritual beings, and I do believe that we come back in other lives. Life's not without its challenges, there's still lots to be done and once you get to experience the momentum of having these incredible experiences just happening time and time again, the negative stuff that happens just pales in comparison. That allows me to operate at a place of gratitude and enjoyment in life - far more than most people that I meet - but I have an obligation to be able to share that experience so that other people can experience and destroy a lot of their limiting beliefs. I had to, out of necessity, become bold, fearless, and courageous when it came to reaching out and connecting with my heroes in order to bring them on to the podcast, or drum up business when

I worked in my former career in recruitment. That adversity was very painful at the time, but it has become this wonderful gift, and also a really amazing revenue stream. I think that's the thing that I really want people to take away from this is: I can live this life that I've only watched on TV, and I've got it all within me.

How Can People Work with You?

There are two resources that I want to make available. One is especially for people that have been seriously thinking about creating their own platform, whether it be a podcast and YouTube channel, or streaming on some other platform. We'd love to give them a head start to avoid maybe two years of pain that I endured, and that's available at 'podcasting.heroes.com.' For everything else, just go to my website at labanditchburn.com. It's got links through to the podcast and the book. I have very limited one-on-one coaching available, but depending on the circumstance and availability, there might be opportunities there as well, because there's just a number of really amazing resources on there that you can use for free to start you on this journey. When I started, I was absolutely and utterly destitute, having nearly gone bankrupt four times in 2019. I needed to be even more resourceful than I am now when it came to learning and healing from the stuff, so you don't need a lot of money to get it started. You just need to know 'Why.'

Words of Wisdom

I'm going to steal another quote from Les Brown. He says, "What people think of me is none of my spiritual business."

By Laban Ditchburn

https://www.LabanDitchburn.com

Uncovering Your Superpower Through Spiritual Transformation

By Laura Staisiunas

Tell Us Your Story

I have a background in clinical pharmacy and have gradually evolved into what I do now - I am a Master Akashic Record consultant and teacher. Additionally, I am an intuitive artist. A lot of people think you have to get struck by lightning and have this huge epiphany when you undergo a transformation. Mine was very slow, and it was filled with ease and grace because my Spirit knew exactly the steps I needed to take to transform into my new 'self'. I grew up on the southside of Chicago in a very traditional Catholic family setting. I have five siblings, and I always knew I wanted to be in the healing field. I'd always been good in science and math, I loved it. That was my passion. That was my adrenaline. That was my rush. That was my focus. That's what I wanted to do, and I was healing people. I was always encouraged by my family and guidance counselors to use my love of healing, science, and math to go into pharmacy.

I followed that path for years because it made sense to me. In the Pharmacy world, I worked in all facets, but I never found my passion. The reason I stayed in my lane was that I was extremely good at what I did. This is what I was told you were good at. It is best for you to do this. This was my zone of excellence.

However, that was not my soul calling, and I had to shake off the programming and leave that tribe for a while. Looking back, this is what you did. You got a good job and continued to do it for the remainder of your life - play it safe. No, you did not change careers. And heaven forbid, you went into some kind of alternative medicine field; it was just not the thing to do. Energy was shifting in me in small steps. Dream analysis was the starting point for me. Then I learned how to read auras and realized that everything is energy. My connection to energy laws, especially the first and second laws of energy, was instantaneous. This felt right at home to me! This led me to seek certification in past life regressions from Dr. Brian Weiss. I was then introduced to the Akashic Records, sacred geometry, and quantum field. I was able to do healing in the Akashic Records and as I learned it's not only information that comes through but it's guidance, wisdom, as well as healing. Rather than a big spiritual explosion (like getting hit by lightning), there were several small segments all linked together. My shamanic work brought me back into harmony with nature, seeing the Divine in all living things. After years of being a hardcore scientist in one world, I discovered the unseen world equally. There was no doubt in my mind that was where my heart was. The familiar energy just resonated with me. My business does exactly that. Working with people who are ready to step into their healing and reach their highest potential is my mission.

Did You Struggle with Judgment?

I was fortunate that my siblings and parents were supportive of my work. My family didn't understand a lot of what I was doing, especially the shamanic work. I tried explaining what I was doing and letting them see what I was doing. There was nothing hidden, everything was open and transparent. Compared to others, they seem to be pretty open. Once I found my spiritual group, I had their support and more doors opened. Due to the international nature of today's world, people are looking for community and support because other means of building a sense of belonging have been invented.

How Did You Get Through the Process?

While working in traditional healthcare and in a lot of large pharmaceutical companies and hospitals, I never really revealed my alternative intuitive side. Back then, I was still very selective about who I told about my work with energy fields. A colleague in my department told me, 'Oh, I can't work with this person.' My instinct said, 'You two probably had a past life together and there is an issue you need to resolve.' She said, 'Don't talk about that. It scares me.' So, I thought, okay, step back and be a little bit more discerning. Several years have passed, and now I am broadcasting this story! So, the key for me is discernment.

What Would You Say to Someone in Your Situation?

I see this question asked a lot in the Akashic readings and the coaching that I do. Usually, we open their Akashic records, but sometimes it might just be an intuitive session. Nevertheless, much of this can be attributed to old beliefs and patterns. You have an old limiting belief system and it's often held in one's energy field. You might have societal and ancestral limitations that are still in the subconscious that need to be brought out and cleared. Some of this is held in the body. Your body is so smart, it has body wisdom. Something may have happened in childhood and it's still in the cells. When I does a reading, I can visualize the little mitochondria, and I can see if there's a knot or a visual cue, or maybe the whole segment of the DNA strand is inactive and we need to energetically light that up. I pull a lot of my science into my readings, which is great because I know the body systems so well. It's amazing how much can get cleared if you're ready, and spirit never gives you more than what you can handle. When I work with someone their spirit team might just say, let's do something creative. It might be let's create your own personal deck, and maybe it's only eight cards, but that's healing, unraveling, and unwinding the belief. We might create a ritual for the limiting belief clearing. So, it depends because every person is different. That's really what you have to remember too. I always say my mantra when I work with people; 'Let's discover the undiscovered: YOU.'

What is the Gift?

I think it's being an example for others, because in the beginning, I didn't have the confidence to do this. My unique gifts and talents resonate with the right people, and those people find me. Being of service continues when they too are an example for others. There are so many people doing what I'm doing, and it's all about who you resonate with, and who you are in alignment with. I'm honest with people; I tell them to take whatever resonates and leave the rest. The universe will give you the messages you need and sometimes you're only ready to receive 10% at the time but then six months later, they're ready for the rest of the guidance given to them.

What do You do for People?

I call myself an intuitive healer because I feel people have the capacity to heal themselves. What I do is distill everything that I have learned and experienced, together with all my teachings in helping them find their own inner healer. Each session is something different and I'm able to distill, for example, that this person needs a shamanic guide to come in, or this person needs a creative activity to do, whatever it takes to really anchor in what this person needs. I'm able to assimilate all of this. It might be a shamanic art journey; I don't know but something always comes through. But I'm open to receive information for them, and that's what I get told to do.

Words of Wisdom

Say yes to transformation, no matter what it is, say yes to your superpower. Sometimes we don't even know what our superpower is, but if you're in alignment trust your True Self; you'll find it. Maybe my purpose for that one particular day is to help just one particular person - so that's my superpower of the day. We're not meant to be sitting and meditating all day long, it's getting out there and being of service, connecting with others.

More about Laura

Laura is an intuitive, creative, and earth-honoring practitioner. It is her gift to blend these gifts into teaching others how to bring light into their everyday lives. By exploring sacred sites throughout the world, Laura gained a deeper understanding of her own gifts and talents. Her creative soul art pieces and workshops reflect those experiences. Using her practical approach, she delves into areas of limiting beliefs, feelings of powerlessness, being stuck, relationships, and health issues in helping her clients' find true power of freedom.

She accesses the Akashic field for wisdom and guidance to expand one's inner wisdom and well-being. She is certified in intuition, the Akashic records, past life regression, energy healing, gemstone therapy, shamanic studies, and aromatherapy, among other fields as well. Her ability to guide individuals to their highest potential comes from combining these different modalities. In addition to one-on-one sessions and group gatherings, Laura also teaches workshops in person and online.

By Laura Staisiunas

https://www.LittleAspenStudios.com
Email: littleaspenstudios@gmail.com

The Displaced Soul...Oops, I'm in the Wrong Body and Embracing Your Divine Soul

By Lois Warnock

Tell Us Your Story

I'm going to try and keep this humorous because that's how I got through my life of interesting events as I put it. I was looking at the outline for my book, which is called, 'The Displaced Soul…Oops, I'm in the Wrong Body and Embracing Your Divine Soul.' That encapsulates my whole journey to where I am today. In looking at the chapter outlines, I thought, you need to have grit if you want to live in a family with nine siblings. I called myself a very middle child. Because I was number six and I felt like I was the mediator all the time, but also as a child I felt displaced, and I don't really know that I even understood it. I just know that I used to say to my mom that I think I'm in the wrong family. I don't think I'm supposed to be here. I think I'm supposed to be somewhere else. And she would shoosh me out the door and just say go play with your sisters and brothers, but they don't want to play with me. I'm in the middle - I'm not in the older group and I'm not in the younger group - so I did tend to entertain myself.

I have had so many experiences, so not all of them are here. I've experienced domestic violence. My first near-death experience was as a child of six or seven when I almost drowned. Another near-death experience with a poisonous spider bite in Arizona, where I was talking to my angels and going down the tunnel. Also, a vehicle accident where I totaled the vehicle when I hit a deer broadside at night and then walking away without a scratch because my airbag didn't go off. I remember calling for help, and I remember a bright light, and there were no other vehicles around, so I knew the lights were coming from elsewhere. In addition, twenty years ago I got hit with a severe lung infection with bronchitis and pneumonia. And here we are, twenty years later and I'm still battling my breath. I wake up every morning saying thank you, I'm still breathing. I get another day to go play in my art studio, coach or do what calls to me. As a child, I suffered from these horrendous migraines and they never had all the medical tech stuff that they have today, so you just got put in a room for a day or two in the dark with a hot compress and that's how they managed them. I suffered with them through my whole life until I realized, after I started my spiritual journey, all of a sudden, my migraines went away. I started to look at that and wonder what that is. Five years into my 'lung issue' I was very unhappy with traditional medicine, and a friend of mine said why don't you take Reiki and see if you can teach that body how to heal itself. I'm always willing and open to try anything, so I began my energy healing journey and today I have three Reiki Masters. I began my two-year Crystal Resonance Practitioner Certification. It was a very intense and healing journey, and it was then that I did meditative studies. I tried to learn as much as I could about the energy of the body.

Part way through that I got invited to go on a spiritual journey. I just knew I had to go and when I went and studied with this amazing woman, who was teaching about the Masters of the Far East, spiritualist teachings and more, I experienced a profound transformation. She stood in front of me and said, 'your master says you're a spiritual psychic artist.' I went, 'what the heck is that?' I got told to be quiet and that I really wasn't listening properly several times. So, I listened, and I came home after two weeks and went wow, what is that about? And I thought, either I can go back to my previous normal or I can take the leap. I decided to leap! Several years later as I was continuing my spiritual journey and moving from bureaucratic jobs in government and not for profit, I still struggled with my health and questioned whether all this energy healing was working. Then I had a visit from the breast cancer gene, which is in our family. I actually wasn't expecting the diagnosis because I had just done a routine screening and they saw something. They did a biopsy and then they lost the biopsy. About three weeks later, I got a call from my doctor who asked me to come in, and she said, I'm really sorry, you have stage three cancer, and it's already in your lymph nodes. I thought, that's really annoying. I have a lot of stuff on my plate, and I don't have time for this. She looked at me and said, 'you need to make time for this; this isn't optional.' So off I went to deal with that, among other life events. My daughter was having our grandbaby the same week of my diagnosis. And then my father, who had lived a very long life, was in the last stages and we knew he was going to be departing this physical life. There was just a lot of stuff going on, and me still in that resistance of the cancer diagnosis, so I went on our planned cruise. When I came back, the journey began for the next year with the traditional chemo, surgery and radiation. It was while I was recuperating in Arizona that I got bitten by a poisonous spider.

That gave me another year of healing and trying to deal with all the medical stuff. It's not just about the healing, it's going into these places that are so overwhelming to get treatment. I think the main point was that I wanted to tell my story. Looking back, if I hadn't been doing the energy healing and the crystal healing, I don't think my body would have been ready. I now recognized that as an energy healer, I learned that I actually was taking on everybody's energy since I was a child. I would feel so sad for them, but I never knew that I didn't have to, and that I could feel sad but let it go. All my life I would feel the emotions from others and as a mediator, and I would take on everybody's energy, but not understand that I had to let it go or even how to let it go.

I work a lot with clients to really look at their foundation, provide energy healing, and then do this coaching through spirit. The spirit guides come through and that's been an amazing journey of being able to see spirit, draw spirits and channel all the messages for people, because they're all around us, cheering us on, wanting to help us in our physical life journey.

How Did You Get Through It?

I always had a faith in something bigger than me. I was brought up in a strong religious environment, although I questioned that as I got into spirituality. It doesn't matter what it is, it's the knowledge that there's something bigger than us, and we're part of this journey. Some days I didn't do so well getting through it, and I'm sure I sat and wondered what the heck I was doing when I went through the really dark parts, I gotta listen up. We can choose to stay, or we can choose to go, and sometimes we don't have that choice. This is whatever you believe in, but it was really about owning what I have and that we all have these unique gifts and abilities that need to be shared with the world to help.

When doing some energy work, and the question is in five years, what would you hope to see if you could change one thing? I would like to see world peace. Wouldn't that be amazing? As a kid, I wanted everybody to be happy. I wanted everybody to come up with some sense of it's not exactly what I wanted, but I'm okay with it. So, you just put one foot in front of the other and keep going. Some of these adversities that people have dealt with, they haven't had a choice, but they have a choice of how they're going to deal with it. The more experiences we have, the more we can teach, share, and help others because we're all helping.

What is the Gift?

I have had many, but the gifts right now for me is that because of the adversities I get to do what I love, which is art. It's brought me to this place of being an artist sharing my art; intuitive arts, and psychic art. That's the gift in all of this, and also because I choose to just keep moving forward. I know that I am right where I'm supposed to be and just sharing a story of the spiritual realm with people. Be curious.

I have a book coming out, and it's a commitment. I started with creating a deck of spirit guides and their messages. With my knowledge of crystals, I've incorporated the crystals into the cards. From there, I wanted to do a journal and then I thought, well, maybe I should be writing a book? My book is called 'The Displaced Soul...Oops, I'm in the Wrong Body', Embracing Your Divine Soul. It's about how I went through life thinking maybe I was in the wrong body. In reality, I am in the right body, but there's more on that in the book. It's also about that ceiling, where we feel not balanced or we feel that something is off kilter and how to embrace our divine soul. We're not all meant to do the same things and thank goodness because we'd be pretty boring. It's about embracing who you are, embracing the body that you have, and how it's carried you through this thing called life. I have a lot of different chapters in there about my experiences but really, I want to take it back to how all those experiences can help you to really look at whether you have to rebuild your foundation. I talk about the energetic healing part of whatever has happened and how you can do that. In the processing of that, it gives you tools, so that's what I hope my book will do for people. It's also to make them curious, because that's how we learn and that's how we experience, by being curious.

Words of Wisdom

If you're feeling out of sorts, pick up a packet of crayons or pencils. Download your favorite picture or mandala and just color. Just be in that energy of what you have right in front of you. Don't think about chasing away all that other stuff, just concentrate on what's right in front of you.

By Lois Warnock

www.LoisWarnock.com loiswarnock@telus.net

Following a 30-year business career, she chose to pursue the 'energy healing' field in 2005, after a debilitating chronic lung condition. Since then she has obtained several Reiki Master designations in Usui-Angelic-Spiritual Reiki; Crystal Resonance Therapy Certification™, Advanced Meditative studies in Primus Healing Techniques™ and Advanced Angel Empowerment Practitioner Certifications. These teachings provided an incredible vibrational healing for her. On a spiritual trek to Alaska in 2012, she was introduced to the Spiritualist teachings and her Master Teacher in Spirit. This was the beginning of her 'soul mission' of Spiritual Psychic Art. She has drawn over 1,000 spirits for clients around the globe, as she channels messages through her mediumship. She continues to share her story of overcoming adversity, her spiritual discipline and providing others with tools for their spiritual journey. She is currently working on her own book "The Displaced Soul - Oops I'm in the Wrong Body...embracing your divine soul", where she shares her story of overcoming adversity by connecting to one's spiritual guides.

Surviving Childhood Trauma and Thriving: A Personal Journey

By Mary Black

Tell Us Your Story

I was finally going to write a book about my personal journey as a child of alcoholic parents, and the emotional, physical, and sexual abuse. I was the oldest of five and there was a lot that fell on my shoulders. My book is going to be entitled 'Why Did I Survive?' Surviving childhood trauma and thriving, because that has been a question that I have asked myself my whole life. I realized that with a lot of soul searching, and inner reflection, I realized that all these experiences shaped my life and those around me. Being forced into certain situations and circumstances really did make me the person that I am today. In trying to understand how I got healthy, and the realization that it took a lot of people along the way to help me, I learned how to identify why I reacted to certain events that resulted in anger, fear, lack of trust, dislike of uncertainty, control issues and grief. It also produced the ability to survive and actually thrive throughout my life. At a young age, I noticed that my family wasn't like others. At first, I thought they were weird, but it was actually my family that was different, and I did have to grow up pretty fast because there were a lot of responsibilities on my shoulders. When I was in third grade, my grandfather had died, my baby brother - who was a month old – had meningitis and was in a coma, and my mom had a nervous breakdown. That's when all of the responsibilities and chores of the home were on me. I didn't realize at the time that the anxiety, distress, fearfulness and hopelessness that I was experiencing was caused by all those chores I had to do. I just knew I had to keep going and pushing forward no matter what, because my siblings were counting on me. I don't remember what directed me to reach out to my middle school counselors for help, but there I was, and I learned transactional analysis and coping skills. Unfortunately, they had notified my parents that I had reached out which of course led to beatings, but they continued to help me anyhow, which I'm so grateful for. I loved being at school, and I excelled. I was in AP classes through middle school and high school. I could have graduated years earlier, but I had no place to go. I participated in the school basketball, baseball, and swim team, and I was part of an elite women's singing group and on the debate team. I also worked a twenty-four hour a week job, since I was fifteen and a half. I don't know if I did that just to keep me busy, but that's what happened. There were many other incidents during my childhood that were terrifying and bizarre that I won't get into, but just know that it was a roller coaster. Beatings were frequent, and Chris and I had welts and scars that are still a reminder today. The verbal attacks and name-calling were unrelenting, constantly letting me know I was worthless and that I wasn't going to amount to anything. As a child I was hospitalized over thirteen times due to neglect and resulting in convulsions.

At one point, I died when they coded me back, and it was my sister that got help from our neighbor to take me to the hospital because my mom was too drunk. I never learned to cry, but all I wanted to do was to scream into a pillow when things got out of control. In 1969, at age fifteen, while my mother was beating me out of nowhere, I grabbed her arm and told her that I would deck her if she hit me again. I never forgot the look of fear and shock in her eyes. I walked out of the house to the police station and asked the chief of police for help. I don't know what made me do it, but I think I just had enough. Miraculously he did get me to social services, but back in 1969, it was unheard of for a child to take their parents to court. I don't even think there was a juvenile court back then. The judge didn't know what to do. They did assign an attorney to me. The whole process took over three months, and throughout it, I just cried. My parents of course were angry and embarrassed and were more concerned about what other people were going to think of them. I had teachers, clergy and scout counselors that testified for me. The judge had never had a child petition the court to be removed from them, and he didn't know what to do, so a psychological evaluation was ordered in the hope of making that decision easier for him. It was their recommendation that I be removed from the home for my physical and emotional well-being. They also wanted me to get individual and group therapy so that I wouldn't feel guilty, but I didn't understand what that meant until I was older. So, the judge did decide to follow the psychological evaluation and I was placed into foster care. I did receive the individual and group counseling, and my parents were ordered to as well, but they didn't comply. Foster care was a safe place for me, but it was also a very lonely place. I felt like I really didn't fit in. I also couldn't see my siblings so that was very hard. I turned eighteen and in December of my senior year, foster care ended. My school counselor rented out his basement to me until I graduated and went into the army. I felt the army would be a good way for me to decide if medicine was the field that I wanted to pursue as a career. I was trained as a medic and an ENT specialist. I did graduate at the top of the class at the Academy of Health Sciences, and I was assigned to them. After the army, I used my GI Bill to get my Registered Nursing degree. Nursing was very fulfilling for me, I enjoyed the challenge, and helping others of course. My second sister died of bulimia and drug abuse at the age of thirty-two. Sister number one - who was about a year and a half younger than me - became delusional manic bipolar and committed suicide at the age of forty-nine. My sister number three - the baby of the family - died at forty-two from alcohol and drug abuse, and my only brother to this day suffers from deep depression, low self-esteem and suicidal isolation. I was so angry, wanting to know why I made it and they didn't or couldn't. I always sought out therapy to help throughout my life, when certain things would trigger symptoms of anxiety, or physical symptoms like diarrhea, nausea or headaches. I remember having a panic attack during a lecture in nursing school when they were discussing child abuse, and I couldn't understand what was happening to me until I realized it was a trigger. When I graduated from college, I had been told throughout my life that I wasn't going to amount to anything and that triggered the reaction from me because I had a piece of paper saying that I did make something out of my life. When my son was born, many events triggered symptoms. I was so determined to break the cycle that I learned how to identify those reactions and triggers, and I listened to my body and sought help when needed. It took a while to learn how to do that, but I did. I started my own business and reached the top of that profession within a year while I was working full time as a registered nurse and administrator. I had two part time jobs, did scuba diving during summer months, and I was commuting three hours a day. Any obstacle or challenge I had I just never gave up, and I would find a way over it, under it, around it, through it - legally of course - until I succeeded. Even with all that success, I was always bothered by how I survived. I still had anger wanting to know why. Why can't everyone overcome and make something of their lives instead of giving up and turning to alcohol and drugs and unhappiness? By writing this book I've learned even more about myself, and I realized that I had the ability to see things from the outside looking in. I was always curious, and I believed that by participating in all the school activities, I developed self-confidence without needing approval or support from anyone. I never had anyone in the audience encouraging me or even just watching me - even at graduation - I did it for me. I'm still writing this book and hopefully they'll finish soon. I am grateful for healing and answering some of my why questions, and I hope that I can help others with their journey. Many times, I wonder what would my life be like today if I had great parents who encouraged and loved me when I went to MIT and developed a cure for cancer or some other incredible medical breakthrough? What would my life have looked like? But I also realized, yeah, my life would be different. But would I be where I am today, happy, content, and traveling around the world experiencing the wonders. What if I never developed that drive to never give up? I know those trials and tribulations that I went through actually shaped and directed my life, and I'm okay with that because I liked the outcome. There were turning points in my life that really made a big difference with the counselors in school, and church of course. As a young adult, I had read this book called 'Children of Alcoholics: a Survival Manual,' which was a real eye opener to me. It described in detail each one of my siblings and my parents so much that it gave me goosebumps all over my body. There was another book I can't remember the title of, but the one phrase of that book that really has helped me throughout my life, said the only person that can make you upset is you; and that was pretty profound. I realized the value of books and how they helped me, and I'm hoping that other people will be able to identify similar situations, help them navigate their lives to a healing place, seek out safety and happiness, and to overcome and excel.

How Did You Get Through It?

I have this inner drive or this inner strength that just made me keep pushing on. I think the curiosity that I always had about things really made a big difference. And I just never gave up; I wanted to be happy.

What Would You Tell Someone in a Similar Position?

I would say, learn to slow down and enjoy the things around you. Look at the birds, look at the buds on the trees. Look at the cloud's formations. Just look at the wonder that surrounds you. Also, it's okay to be selfish sometimes. That was hard for me. To learn self-help and self-care is very important because you can't be everything to everybody all the time. Try to remove the toxic environment and the toxic people in your life and learn when to walk away. It's okay to not talk to them for the rest of their lives. Why - if you put your hand in a fire and it burns - would you keep sticking your hand in the fire? It makes no sense. So just learn to remove yourself from those toxic situations and let go of things you can't control. There are some things you can control and there's some things you can't and remember that the only person who can make you upset is you. I choose happiness, living life to its fullest, and helping others. It provides energy and joy to me, and I think by helping others, you feel yourself. Right now, I'm a full-time caregiver to my husband and have a lot of challenges there. I'm really trying to do the self-care stuff. I get massages twice a month and that keeps me from being arrested for attempted homelessness. I haven't been able to spend as much time as I would like, so I have partnered with a friend who's writing a book on poems and things like that. We try to meet once a month to keep us on track.

What's Your Superpower?

I think it's curiosity and wanting to save other people where I couldn't save my siblings, although I tried. I tend to want to save people around me that are less fortunate.

By Mary Black

email: blackandcoal@aol.com

Rising Strong: A Pathway to a Vibrant Life

By Michelle Abraham

Tell Us Your Story

I'm going to take you guys way back to when I was a teenager graduating high school. I had the fortunate opportunity to represent Canada with girl guides in the summer between grade 10 and grade 11. I was chosen as the one girl to represent British Columbia and then went with 10 other girls representing different provinces across Canada. We spent three weeks at The Girl Guide place in Switzerland and I fell in love with Switzerland. It was the coolest place ever. Between that and a trip to Italy in grade 11 for our school social studies program, I was hooked on both Europe and traveling. During my year 12 of high school, I was looking at what I wanted to do for school and realized that the program that I really wanted to take was called outdoor recreation, business management. It was a lot of hiking, backpacking, and kayaking. The problem with the program was that they only take 30 kids a year and you had to be 19 years old, so I wasn't old enough. I really wanted to get into the school, but I didn't want to just go take English, Geography, or something for the heck of it. I convinced my counselor at school to help me find somewhere to go that was fun and exciting. She hooked me up with a family that was looking for an au pair or nanny who lives with a family. The day after I graduated high school, I got the job with a family in Switzerland. Living with this family was an interesting experience being integrated into a different culture. The husband was from Canada, so he could relate to a little bit of the struggles I was having. They have a higher standard of things in Switzerland, like having to be dressed up to be a nanny, I couldn't just wear my sweats. I had a wonderful year and made all sorts of great friends because every family had to have an au pair. My life was on a high and my two friends from high school decided that they're going to come and spend the summer backpacking around Europe. We had plans to go to about 12 different countries in a matter of eight weeks, so I was excited when they showed up on my doorstep in Switzerland. We went to Germany, the Netherlands, England, France, the Czech Republic and then went back to the south of France. On August 11th, 1999, my friend and I walked out to this circle in the middle of the ocean one day, sat down, and wrote down all the cool things that we wanted to do on another trip. This time we were going to go to Africa, Central America, and South America. Once we wrote this all down, we dated it, we signed it and then that day we learned that there was a solar eclipse. So, there we were in the early hours of the morning watching the solar eclipse. That morning we were sitting out there watching this solar eclipse happen. Later that evening we went out to dinner in Monaco, checking out the lights and nightlife before we were going to catch the train home. My other friend and I decided we were going to head back because she wasn't feeling well and I'd broken my toes playing volleyball in Greece a few days beforehand, so I couldn't walk very well and didn't want to miss the train. We left our other friend Cecilia with some people that we had just met traveling and said we would meet her back at the hospital. My friend Robin and I go back to the hospital. In the middle of the night, there was a knock on the door. You'll need to come with us. There's been an accident. and it was like when I open the door and we're like, oh, open the door. Okay, what's happening? She's like, you have to come with us. There's been an accident. I remember back to before we went out for dinner that night. I was out on the balcony and my brain was wandering. I had this premonition of an accident happening and we were going to have to pack up all the bags and go home. And then I snapped out of that premonition, thinking that was weird. I grabbed her belongings, and we went off to the hospital, but they didn't speak very good English, and we didn't speak very good French. We walked into the hospital room, and we saw the guy that we'd been traveling with sitting there crying, and our friend was nowhere to be seen. With some miscommunication and some back and forth, we found out our friend had been hit by a train that night, and the two of them had missed the last train home to the hospital. They had walked through a tunnel all the way home, thinking that they'd missed the last trains and not realizing that France has trains going through all the time at Mach speed. As they went through a tunnel, a train was coming, and she went one way, and he went the other way. He was totally fine, and she was killed. That moment changed the trajectory of my life. And I know now that she's been with me all this time and helping me create the life that I have now and helping me help other people get their voice out there. I learned at 19 that you don't know how long you have to live and to make the most of what you do have on this earth. I spent many years avoiding healing by distracting myself with lots of adventures and bungee jumping and skydiving and living life to the extreme, because you don't know how long you have. I miss her a lot, but there are so many lessons I learned from her in that short amount of time that we were together. I see signs of her, and I hear her with me all the time. She really helped form and shape the business that I have today and the need to help people get their voice out there in the world because they have a message that they can't leave this earth without conveying it. I've done a lot of healing recently because I usually get really emotional when I tell that story, and now I don't feel as emotional because I know that she's always looking out for me. It was a tough thing to experience at 19 years old, but it's put my life on a trajectory of knowing that there's so much more to living and life. Live it without regrets and without wishing you had done something that you didn't do, or doing something that you wish you had.

How Did You Get Through This?

I traveled a lot, and I think that was my way of being home. I think it was easier for me to continue venturing to other countries and other places. I never actually did that whole list of things that we'd signed earlier that morning before she passed. I didn't have the courage to take that exact trip, but I did continue traveling because I think for me it was easier to be away and meeting new people and having fun and doing those crazy adventures than it was to be at home. It took me a lot of years and it wasn't until I started speaking, doing podcasting, and sharing that story that I was able to heal, so evolving out loud.

What Would You Tell Others Going Through a Similar Situation?

I would tell them that everything's going to be okay. That person had a mission here on earth, they completed that, and that's why they left. Now they're here as your cheerleader on the other side to support you in whatever you're doing. So just know that you have support and backup and they're watching over you as you go through your life.

What is the Gift?

I think the overall gift is learning that life is short. From a young age, I had not really learned that lesson. I probably would have settled for mediocre or settled for a life that was okay, but because I saw how short and how quickly life can be taken away, not taking things for granted and not settling for something that you don't absolutely love in your life has been really important for me. You don't know the hand that you're holding until you don't have that choice anymore. So go and do all the things that you want to do and don't leave anything on a bucket list for when you're 80 years old.

Words of Wisdom

You have an opportunity every day that you wake up. You have a new opportunity to live the life how you imagined it. There's that Henry Thoreau quote, 'Go confidently in the direction of your dreams and live the life you've always imagined.' This was a quote that my parents put in my graduating yearbook, and it's a quote that's been always in my heart. Go confidently in the direction of your dreams and each step that you take moves you closer to reality. Going confidently in that direction and knowing that you have the world at your fingertips, you can unfold this amazing vibrant life. We've now created a life through taking steps towards what we wanted, and this is what I want to leave everyone with today.

How Can Someone Work with You?

If you have a message that you're just dying to get out there in the world, we are the team that can do it for you. We work with people who have a positive impact message that they want to get out there in the world. We help you not only launch your show, but we then manage it for you so that you can just concentrate on doing the recording of what you do best. Our company Amplifyou has launched over 400 shows in the last few years, and we've been doing this for about 10 or 11 years. We absolutely love helping get your message out there in the world by creating a podcast that works to also fulfill your business. So, we're using the podcast as an integral tool that can open doors to relationships to grow your business. I also have a business called aligned adventures where we take those amazing podcasters, coaches, authors, speakers, entrepreneurs and we travel and mastermind and create content.

By Michelle Abraham

Podcast Pioneer | Entrepreneur | High Vibe Visionary 🎙

High Vibe Leaders Mastermind & Aligned Adventures

Amplifying your Voice, Vision & Visibility with Masterminds & Aligned Adventures that Raise Your Vibe, Align Your Business and Nourish Your Soul. Michelle Abraham is a Podcast Pioneer and Entrepreneur known for her high-vibe approach to life and business. As the founder of Amplifyou, North America's top podcast management company, Michelle has launched hundreds of podcasts, earning accolades like Entrepreneur of the Year and Top 50 Moms in Podcasting. With a passion for podcasting, she's on a mission to amplify voices, spark visions, and elevate visibility in the world of entrepreneurship. Join her on this transformative journey! ✸

www.michelleabraham.com

www.contentcreationcamp.net

Resilience Unleashed: Embracing Challenges, Bold Decisions, and the Pursuit of Clarity

By Mike C-Roc

Tell Us Your Story

Life is full of challenges, and while mine have been tough, I know others have faced even harder ones. What sets us apart is how we deal with these hurdles. When I was growing up, my parents were apart, and I spent every other weekend in a different family setting. It wasn't the typical family life. I saw a lot of problems around me—people dealing with alcohol, drugs, anxiety, and strained relationships. Without realizing it, I soaked up all this experience like a sponge. Over time, I realized that these challenges weren't just burdens; they were opportunities. I learned from them, they motivated me, and they became the fuel I needed to keep moving forward. As I got older, I made it a point to share what I'd learned with others to help them improve their lives. I could talk for hours about the challenges I've faced, but I prefer to see them as chances to learn and grow. My early years were spent in a tough environment where people often hurt themselves with drugs, alcohol, and their own emotions. I saw fights, conflicts, and people struggling to get along. It was a difficult backdrop for my youth. But I used these experiences to propel myself into the business world. Navigating the business world was like trying to find your way through a maze. It was challenging to figure out who to trust and who to keep away from. My journey eventually led me to write a book I named "Rocket Fuel." "Rocket Fuel" isn't just a book; it's a testament to how setbacks can be turned into something powerful. At its heart is the 'Rocket Fuel Law,' a simple but profound idea. Instead of letting life's problems weigh you down and slow your progress, you can turn them into fuel for your journey. In these pages, you'll discover how to transform setbacks into the energy you need to move forward. Every obstacle can become a source of motivation and drive, pushing you to achieve more than you ever thought possible. This is the essence of my journey—the belief that challenges are opportunities waiting to be turned into your power source for an extraordinary life.

How Do You Help People Who Come to You?

I often find myself in conversations with individuals who feel lost, unsure of their next steps, or trapped in the labyrinth of their problems. In those moments, I make one thing crystal clear: it's perfectly fine not to have all the answers, but it's not okay to declare yourself as "stuck." You see, when you label yourself as such, you're inadvertently weaving a story around your identity—'I am stuck.' But are you truly stuck, or are you a vibrant human being, a spiritual entity, merely tangled in a temporary challenge? This is where our journey begins, disentangling the threads of self-imposed limitation and examining what led you to utter those words—'I am stuck.' We must scrutinize what we attach to the powerful words 'I am.' Then, we delve deeper, uncovering the roots of your feelings. What lies beneath the surface? What experiences, beliefs, or fears contribute to this sense of entrapment? But we don't stop there. Instead, we pivot our focus towards clarity. What if you could dream without boundaries, envisioning the ideal life where limitations and barriers cease to exist? Who would be by your side? Where would you reside? What experiences would fill your days? It's imperative to define these aspirations in vivid detail, not merely as dreams but as daily intentions. I often share a formula that has shaped my own path and countless others': intention dictates attention. What you intend to manifest guides where you place your focus. As you attend to these intentions, they gradually gain validation, ultimately becoming tangible realities in your universe. Consider the universe itself—a vast cosmos that encompasses us all. We inhabit this common space, yet each of us molds our individual universe. The scope of your universe, its grandeur, and its composition hinge on your perception, driven by intention. This is the crux of the matter. Many find themselves adrift because their intentions remain muddled or absent. They wonder why their lives lack the desired results, why they're ensnared in mediocrity, why relationships, finances, and well-being falter. It's all connected to intention—or the lack thereof. When you drift without intention, you unwittingly subject yourself to the intentions of others or the aimless scattering of your own attention, which all too often gravitates toward negativity. So, the path to transformation begins with a crystal-clear intention. Through this lens, you can rewrite your narrative, sculpt your destiny, and cease living by default. Instead, you become the master of your own universe, where intention shapes attention, validation solidifies it, and existence is redefined. In clarity lies the power to break free from the shackles of uncertainty, to awaken your purpose, and to illuminate the path to an extraordinary life.

What Would You Say About People Always Bringing the Negative into Their Lives?

In life, the choices we make are like building blocks that construct our reality. Think about it: when we face setbacks, failures, or moments of discouragement, we often respond with decisions. These decisions, simple or complex, end up carving the path we follow. They define the course of our lives. Consider the thoughts that swirl within your mind daily—the ideas, memories, and emotions. They are all a result of choices you've made in the past. It's what you think, say, and do that creates the world you live in. Your own little universe. But here's the thing: we tend to overlook the incredible power we hold. The constant noise of modern life—the never-ending news, social media, and everyday routines—distracts us from realizing the potential within us. We're conditioned not to see and embrace this amazing ability we all possess. Throughout history, there has been a lingering worry about people discovering this hidden formula of power. Some fear that individuals could become too influential. It's like a story from the Bible that many might recognize. When God's presence shone brightly, people had to shield their eyes from the overwhelming light. Acknowledging this incredible capacity, we have come with a twofold responsibility. On one hand, we can achieve amazing things and shape our lives the way we want. But we also need to be careful because this power can be used for harm if we're not mindful of our choices. Even those who may be considered "evil" usually don't want to cause destruction. It's just that they're not looking beyond the immediate moment, beyond the instant satisfaction of their decisions. They're trapped in a cycle of thoughtless choices that lead to destructive actions. So, as we navigate our life journey, let's not ignore our incredible potential. Instead, let's embrace it with respect and wisdom. The power within us shines brightly, offering endless possibilities. Understanding the profound impact of our choices and how they ripple through our lives can lead us on a path of strength and insight. It's a journey that invites us to rise above the ordinary, to recognize our remarkable gifts, and to use them for good in a world hungry for positive change.

What Would You Say to Someone Who Feels Like They're Bringing Evil into Their Lives?

My response is rooted in the power of choice and emotional transformation. First and foremost, I'd ask them to reflect on what they truly desire in life. Do they genuinely want to perpetuate a pattern of negativity? What kind of life do they envision for themselves? Shifting the focus towards their true desires is the initial step towards change. The next key insight lies in recognizing the connection between emotions and actions. When we find ourselves in the depths of anger, depression, sadness, boredom, antagonism, apathy, or similar negative emotional states, our actions often align with these feelings. We unwittingly enter a destructive mode. However, there's another path—one of emotional elevation. When we manage to rise above the cloud of negativity and reach emotional states of excitement, exhilaration, and happiness, we enter a constructive mode. These positive emotions have the potential to transform our actions and experiences. The journey towards emotional elevation begins with self-awareness. We must delve into our past and scrutinize the decisions we've made, as these decisions shape our belief systems. By revisiting these pivotal moments, we can begin to unravel the patterns that keep us ensnared in negativity. But the crucial catalyst for change is setting clear intentions, goals, and targets aligned with a constructive life. Without a clear path forward, we remain susceptible to destructive tendencies. It's like navigating through a dense forest without a map; we're likely to get lost in the undergrowth of negativity. So, my message is simple yet profound: Choose to elevate your emotions. Cultivate an environment where constructive emotions thrive. Reflect on your past decisions and realign them with your true desires. Set intentions that lead you toward a life filled with positivity and growth. Embrace this transformative journey, for it holds the power to free you from the grip of negativity and lead you towards a brighter, more fulfilling future.

What is the Challenge That You Had to Get Over?

The most recent chapter of my journey presented a significant challenge—a crossroads where the familiar clashed with the uncharted. For seventeen years, I had carved my path in the complex world of real estate and mortgages. Along this journey, I was fortunate to have four of my closest friends as my business partners. Together, we navigated the complexities of our industry and tasted success. Yet, a strong desire brewed within me—an eagerness to go beyond mortgages and enter the realm of a global creative brand. I wanted to empower people to excel in their fields and give them the tools to overcome any obstacle. This venture wasn't just about helping others; it also had the potential for substantial financial gain. But here's the heart of my problem: I clung to the mortgage business because it provided stability and security. This attachment, however, took a toll on me. It weighed heavily on my mind, caused doubt and distraction, and dulled my creativity. Then, about four weeks ago, I reached a crucial moment—an epiphany. I decided to let go of my hold on the familiar, just like releasing a grip on a comforting object. It was a move towards freedom from the indecision that had trapped me for too long. Maybe I would move forward, or maybe I wouldn't. Indecision is chaotic and confusing, stifling clarity and progress. In a candid conversation with my friend Chris, I saw that he was grappling with the same feelings I had. But in that moment, I did something significant; I made a choice. It wasn't without fear, as change often brings uncertainty. However, as I committed to my decision, something amazing happened—the burden that had weighed me down for so long disappeared. The change was clear. A new brightness lit up my path, and the fog of indecision lifted. The 'maybe' that had held me back was replaced by a clear decision, propelling me forward. No longer stuck, I began a journey free from confusion, embracing the exciting prospect of success and personal growth. This chapter is a testament to the power of choice—a choice to let go of the familiar and embrace the unknown, to free oneself from indecision, and to step into the radiant light of clarity. It's in the crucible of decisive action that the seeds of greatness are planted.

How Did You Get Through It?

In my life's journey, one principle stands unwavering and paramount: the power of clarity and unwavering commitment to one's desires. I am a firm believer that to realize one's dreams, it is imperative to define them without restraint and etch them into the tapestry of daily existence. Each day, I embark on a ritual, a ritual of self-affirmation that shapes the man I aspire to be. With unyielding determination, I script my identity in the words, "I am loving, and I am loved. I'm all-powerful. I'm unstoppable. I'm healthy. I'm happy, I'm wealthy. I am I am I am." But it doesn't end there. I delve deeper into this profound declaration, painting vibrant portraits of the life I desire. "I'm a man whose love for his wife deepens with each passing day. Our relationship blossoms in the fertile soil of shared experiences. I am an extraordinary father, nurturing bonds with my children that strengthen ceaselessly. Financially, I envision abundance—an inflow of wealth that exceeds my needs, allowing me to invest in others and create ripples of positive change. My reach extends far and wide, touching lives across the globe. I am a luminary—a movie star crafting hit after hit, a visionary behind a multi-billion-dollar brand. These affirmations are more than mere words; they serve as directives for my life's journey. Through them, I channel my intentions, and my intentions, in turn, guide my attention. It is in the fertile ground of clarity and intention that I sow the seeds of my destiny. But it's not just about intentions; it's about decisions. Decisions are the crucible in which dreams are forged. I have discovered the profound potency of decisive choices. When you decide, you seize control of your destiny. The world becomes your canvas, and you wield the brush. At the crossroads of life, there often lies a path less traveled, a path fraught with difficulty. When the journey becomes arduous, and you feel the weight of uncertainty, do not falter. In those moments, the power of decision beckons. Choose to push forward, to pursue the right path, regardless of the challenges that lie ahead. I fervently advocate for the abandonment of phrases like "figure it out" or "I'm going to try." These phrases, laden with ambiguity, leave room for doubt and the possibility of inaction. Instead, embrace the transformative potential of declaring, "I'm going to do this." This declaration carries with it the weight of commitment and the indomitable spirit of decisiveness. With each decision, you clear the path before you, removing obstacles and unfurling the map to your dreams. The lessons gleaned from past trials become the compass by which you navigate uncharted waters.

What is the Gift?

The gift of decision is that it clears our path, removing obstacles and propelling us toward our goals. Lessons learned from past trials become invaluable tools in our journey forward.

How Can People Work with You?

For those seeking to embark on this transformative journey, you can find me on Instagram @mikeycroc. Through That1 Agency, we connect individuals with podcast opportunities, helping them gain exposure. Our mission goes further; we assist in monetizing that exposure by crafting effective messaging and systems, enabling scaling without squandering valuable opportunities.

Words of Wisdom

In parting, I reiterate the significance of clarity in defining our own destinies. Let us not allow others to dictate our paths or chase foreign goals. By crystallizing our intentions, we can pursue our dreams, embrace unstoppable growth, and live life to its fullest potential.

By Mike C-Roc

mike@peoplebuildinginc.com

https://www.MikeCRoc.com

Finding Courage and Purpose in the Face of Adversity

By Rachelle Babler

Tell Us Your Story

My story of grit, guts, and courage comes from different chapters in my life. I would say one of the biggest hurdles I had experienced in this lifetime was in 2008, when I was diagnosed with a rare brain tumor. During that time, I had a newborn and an eighteen- month-old, and I was married. I was scared and would have done anything and everything to get rid of that thing growing inside my head. I remember going down the dark rabbit holes wondering if my children would know their mother. It was a very scary time for me. It all started when I went to my doctor's appointment, and I was having really bad vertigo and severe dizziness at the end of my pregnancy. They said it would go away after I had my baby, but it didn't; it got worse. My doctor referred me to an ENT specialist who said he thought I should go to physical therapy. I remember telling him, no, that I wanted an MRI. That was where it took a little grit and courage because there can be a huge intimidation factor with the white coat and talking to a doctor. Intuitively we know our body so well so when something isn't right, we must share that and be brave. We had a conversation and he finally agreed to the MRI, which was how they found my brain tumor. Having children and a family gave me grit and courage to fight and get through a challenging, year long process. The brain tumor was growing fast, my insurance denied the treatment I had wanted, and I had to really navigate through many hurdles to get to where I am today, which is almost fifteen years post diagnosis. That was a big challenge for me where I decided to really take control of my thoughts and my actions, which would then lead to really taking care of myself and getting myself to a better place. It wasn't the easiest of times, but when I look back, I think that that time was such a huge gift for me because this was when I dove into my personal development work and started to learn all of these amazing things that I had never done, especially meditation.

How Did You Get Through It?

I just decided that I was going to do everything I could to get rid of it. The type of brain tumor I had was typically benign, so many people live with them for years and not do anything because they won't bother you and typically grow less than a percent a year. Well, mine grew almost 40% in six months, so that's when the red flags came up and they decided that I needed treatment right away. In the midst of all the chaos, I took one thing at a time and just kept asking questions to get me to where I wanted to be. I think one of the biggest lessons for me is that when you feel like you're overwhelmed with a diagnosis, stress in your life or something that's really heavy, remind yourself that inch by inch is a cinch, and yard by yard is hard. A mentor once told me that and it's a great reminder and easy to remember.

What Would You Tell Someone Facing the Same Situation?

I would tell them to listen to their intuition and don't be afraid to ask questions. Don't be afraid to seek options, and don't be afraid that you can't get through this. Our mind is powerful. Looking back, I would have worked on shifting my thoughts more, but I was riddled with fear. I was really focused on my brain tumor which I'm sure didn't help my situation at that time. It's really trying to look outside the box I guess; remember that there are other options if we just widen our lens a little bit. It's during these challenging times where self-care and self-love is a priority. Give yourself grace during that time and don't be afraid to ask for support. There were so many people that came and helped me with my kids during that time and I don't know why we're not as open to receive help, especially when we need it. There is no shame in opening up ourselves, being vulnerable and asking for the support to help us through those difficult times.

What is the Gift?

The gift for me was when I was faced with my own mortality. I live life to the fullest. When I do my weekly prep I ask myself, "If this was my last week on earth, what would I do differently?" My diagnosis taught me to really live life my way; unapologetically. We never know when our time is going to come. The diagnosis was definitely a wakeup call for many things and an awakening to what is serving you in your life and what isn't.

What Do You Do?

I help support a lot of speakers, primarily with their TEDx ideas. We get clear on their "idea" for the stage, messaging for their application content, the framework for their talk and stage prep. That's one facet, and the other is sharing your story through music. My program 'Lyrical Revival' is really about sharing your story through song and advocating for a cause you are passionate about. There's a deep connection between music and people. We've seen that at concerts where everybody comes together and are all united in song; music is very powerful.

What Made You Get into Advocating for Music?

That came after my sister passed away in 2018 from cancer. She died after a two-and-a-half-year battle and the day after she died, I wrote a song about her cancer journey, which really was a way for me to channel my grief. She was 48 years old; she was young. I just channeled my grief into writing, and that writing turned into a song and then I used that song to advocate her story and to bring awareness to colon cancer. I took that idea to the TEDx stage in 2021, which was titled "The Power of Advocating Through Music."

This TEDx talk was one of my most challenging talks because it was so emotionally connected to me. But it was awesome because my goal for doing TEDx was so that if I can help even one person take charge of their health, then I've done my job. I have had several people reach out telling me they got screened, they found precancerous polyps which were removed, but had they not gone, who knows what would have happened? I feel like that purpose has been fulfilled, and a lot of that has to do with my sister's journey. It's that legacy piece of keeping her spirit alive and sharing her story that's continuing to make an impact.

What Is Your Superpower?

I think my superpower is meditating because meditation sparks creativity, is our direct connection to God and channels the answers. It gives me direction, guidance, and helps me to not question "my gut" because meditating strengthens that intuition of ours. Many times, we say that we should have listened to our gut. When you start to nourish that inner voice of yours then you don't question it, and it makes life a lot easier and a lot more fun. Meditation is your internal GPS, and it will guide you through all things in this life.

Words of Wisdom

Tomorrow is not promised, so do you unapologetically. Meditate everyday, commit to it. It will change your life. If you have a goal or a dream, take one step every day to get closer to that. You will create the momentum to get you there.

How Can People Work with You?

They can find me on Instagram, LinkedIn, and my website, RachelleBabler.com. Rachelle Babler is a TEDx speaker, #1 International Best-Selling Co-Author, and Entrepreneur & Advocate who grew up in Southern California. She has had an eclectic background of careers: Paramedic turned Forensic Analyst turned Entrepreneur. After being diagnosed with a rare brain tumor and diving into personal development work, she quit her job cold turkey to pursue her "why" and discovered what that was during a global pandemic. She is a storytelling strategist supporting clients who want to amplify their voice, message and brand through various media platforms such as the TEDx stage and through music. She is grateful she took a leap to create a purpose-driven business and to show her two children, Austin and Camryn, that it's never too late to pursue your dreams.

By Rachelle Babler

www.rachellebabler.com
https://www.linkedin.com/in/rachelle-babler-038952176/

My Story Moved a Mountain
By Tammy Gross

Tell Us Your Story

"Sing while you're young and write when you're old." Guess I turned old around 2008. But I found that the transition, from a business standpoint, was pretty smooth. I got this! As soon as working online had become a possibility in the 1990s, I had started arranging music for churches all around the world, and that taught me that I was a facilitator. I also learned how to get business and bring people to me, because early on I figured out Search Engine Optimization (SEO), which relied on keywords. So, when I started writing and editing, everything operated pretty much the same way as when I'd arranged music. I was always number one in my field by creating something that never existed. However, in 2018, Google changed an algorithm that revolutionized SEO, but no one sent me the memo. It took me about six months to figure out why I was suddenly not getting any clients. It was getting harder to pay my bills. Where was all that money I used to have left at the end of the month? Once I realized what had happened with Google, it took another six months to figure out what to do about it. The answer I kept coming up with was that now it was a content game. SEO was no longer about keywords. And figuring out how to add that kind of creation time to my hours-for-dollars business was stressing me as I found myself in a vicious cycle of wasting more time trying to figure out how to have time to keep my business afloat. As it turns out, I was worrying myself pretty much to death. Some kind of stone developed in my gut, and it was killing me. And their method for getting rid of it almost killed me, because they had to blow it out of my intestinal system. They even told me ahead of time, "You're gonna get pancreatitis now." And that's what I got. Scary. Whenever the pancreas is involved, it's easy to connect how that's the cancer people die from. That microscopic stone sent me down what would be a two-year journey in and out of the hospital, decimating my business in the process. Weakening my spirit along the way. And halfway through my journey, we all plunged into a pandemic. COVID didn't affect me too much as an editor because I was already a professional stay-at-home worker, but it really did change my attitude. I felt like I could do anything before all that happened, but losing my business, being close to death and having no control over anything in the world around me just broke me somehow. And I became a total wimp. Soon after the initial COVID shutdown, Pete Vargas virtually brought together a whole bunch of remarkable people who'd lost everything and then built it up again. Every day I was getting these messages of resilience, and they really had an effect. It changed not only me, but my attitude toward people with these amazing stories. As I reflected on how 2020 was going, and the years leading up to it, I got this word: GRIT. I needed grit again, even though, admittedly, that had been a bit of a negative in my younger days. But now I could see that, like any good protagonist, my weakness could become my strength. I needed that youthful gumption and resilience back. An old word I'd learned while doing research for a screenplay was "indefatigable," used to describe Woodes Rogers, the man who tirelessly and single-handedly rid the Caribbean of piracy in the 18th century. And my tenacious little Boston Terrier reminded me all the time how much I needed my tenacity back. So, I put all that together to get some GRIT:

Gumption

Resilience

Indefatigability

Tenacity

That's what I lived by, and it really changed me. I really did develop that grit and eventually had courage to move on and start living out a courageous life. Sometimes we do get into certain situations where we don't have control. How am I supposed to be strong through this? Everybody else is in control of me right now. I had to just own it and take control.

How Did You Get Through It?

The big word that came out of the COVID situation for us all was "pivot." We've all had to learn to pivot. And it's hard, because most of us don't like change, but I think all of us have learned we have to pivot if we want to keep moving forward. But pivoting doesn't have to mean a new direction. It can be a new way to get around whatever's in the way. In fact, part of having grit is forging forward. The pivot is in the tactics. I still had another year of medical issues to deal with, and I learned that it took courage to get through some painful procedures. That was the hardest one. Courage. Medical staff were great, and they credited me with a calmness in attitude that did not match my pre-pandemic personality at all. Even with the many setbacks I had to endure along the way, it helped to learn an important medical truth: *Our guts and our brains are totally connected.* Go with your gut. A bit of surrender helps give perspective. Once you see the lay of the land, you can strategize a new way of doing things. And that's how I got the courage to move forward. A new point of view. Looking back, especially in this book's context, I got the GRIT because of what I stupidly allowed to ruin my guts, and it took courage to get back on track! Grit, Guts and Courage!

What Is the Gift in Your Story?

Story. That is the gift I found. Story. And that is the gift we all have to give to the world. Stories are powerful. I was telling myself a bunch of nonsense stories. And it changed me in a bad way. I knew I had to make positive changes in my own narrative to survive it all. Along the way, I realized that some of what twists up our guts in knots is complexity. Algorithms are very complex. Processes are complex. The world is complex. Story structure is very…simple. I'd spent decades being told about all the convoluted things that must happen in a song or a story or some other creative work in order for it to be any good. Hogwash! Story is very simple.

Beginning: We start with a problem…

Middle: We climb a mountain of trying and failing…

End: We find a solution.

What gives our stories meaning is that once we've overcome our own mountain, we can now help someone navigate a similar mountain to go from problem to solution really fast. I do a lot of coaching and training now. I wasn't doing that before. I conquered my own mountain with grit, guts and courage, and now I help others do the same with speed and ease.

Words of Wisdom

Life is a journey. That journey has mountains. Mountains are just problems standing in our way. How we solve them is what makes a story worth telling. Tell yours.

Your story can move mountains!

By Tammy Gross

International #1 bestseller, multi-award-winning screenwriter, expert editor & writing coach.

https://reelauthor.com

Gifts:

https://wowhollywood.com/grit

https://wowhollywood.com/mountain

Finding Laughter and Gratitude in the Face of Cancer

By Tammy Rader

Tell Us Your Story

Most showers aren't really that memorable. Think about it. When is the last shower that you remember really well? That's why it's strange to think that it was a shower that changed my life. In January 2021, I was coming out of the shower and combing my long dark hair when I had brushed over my breasts. "Oh, that feels a little weird." I investigated further and felt a lump. I quickly dismissed it, thinking that this was probably nothing since no one in my family has breast cancer. I was wrong. The appointments for a mammogram and ultrasound led to a biopsy, which then led to the phone call in February to confirm, it was indeed breast cancer. The next phone call was from a surgeon to say I needed to have a single mastectomy because it had already spread to my lymph nodes. Devastated is an understatement, as it is for anyone who gets a diagnosis like mine. But that wasn't all. Just a few weeks later, I got *another* phone call where I was told I also had rectal cancer. My mind was blown. When I was sixteen, I was diagnosed with endometriosis and IBS. Over the course of the years, a lot of things happen. Life happens. Stress happens. Marriage, divorce, babies, car accidents, all these things. But at the end of 2019, I was not feeling well. There were 'colors' coming out of me that shouldn't have been coming out of me. I went to get checked out and sure enough, the doctor said I needed to have a colonoscopy and the appointment was booked for April of 2020. Talk about timing, since we all know what happened in 2020. Since the whole world fell apart, so did that appointment. The rectal cancer diagnosis came just fourteen days after I had my first mastectomy, so it's then the journey really began. A lot of grit was required for the treatments. I endured fifty-six rounds of radiation and nine rounds of chemo. The grit was also the pain, it wasn't just about surviving the cancer. It was also about surviving the emotional breakdowns, the anxiety, strains on relationships, losing my hair and being 3000 miles away from my family. My boyfriend was there to support me but when you just want a hug from your mom or your son, it's hard.

What would you say to someone who's just been diagnosed with cancer?

The first thing is to breathe. Take the breaths that you need and just sit and reflect on what you've just heard. I know that may sound bizarre, but everything happens very fast. You need to take a step back and just breathe. Focus on what you can control instead of what you can't control. From that point, as weird or ridiculous as it sounds, *focus on gratitude.* Gratitude is the attitude that will change everything. At this point, having gratitude was simply being able to wake up in the mornings and thanking whomever, whatever, and wherever that I was able to wake up. There were some nights that I went to sleep where I honestly didn't know if I was going to wake up the next morning. I met others that didn't have the will to live in the treatment center, which is hard to see. I thought to myself every day when I had to go for treatments, *I am grateful that I was able to drive myself today. I'm grateful that I'm able to walk in these doors and have my treatments and walk out.* I saw people in wheelchairs and there was no light in their eyes. The fact that there are those that didn't get as far as I am now in my journey is not lost on me. I had the resilience and guts to share my story and to ask for help when I needed it. This was a huge shift for me. I have been a very strong, independent woman who raised her son as a single parent. I didn't ask for help. If I needed something done, I figured out how to do it and I did it. During this process it was hard to ask for help, but it was definitely needed. When you need to ask for help, or if you need the help, ask for it.

What are you doing to get through this?

I always say that my story is a bit of laughter, humor, and gratitude, mixed with a side of cancer. I think of my body as an Airbnb for cancer and I allowed it to come in, I guess, but I kicked it the hell out! I laugh at myself. I can trip over the carpet and laugh. If you need to sit down and go on YouTube and watch a bunch of cats and dog videos or babies laughing, whatever you can do to make yourself laugh. The laughter gives you a break in the moment, in the day, in the hour, or whatever you're needing to get you through. Laughter and gratitude are the two things that have kept me here. Maybe a little stubbornness too.

Are your cancer free now?

I would love to hear those words, but I haven't heard them. Yet. There have been many ups and downs in my journey since I've been done with my treatments. They found some nodes on my thyroid which I had to have biopsied just a few weeks ago. These came back negative, thank goodness. I still have another test, as they also found a polyp on my vocal cords. And a few other issues. While I haven't heard those words yet, I don't believe that there's any cancer in my body. I'm just going to say that. That's how I think I've gotten over all the other hurdles, by thinking that way. I believe that's what kept me on the up and up.

You're doing some work to help people; what are you doing?

I have a new community and it's called BeYOUtiful Beyond Your Diagnosis, by Tam. It's a community of members that have just been diagnosed, are in the middle of their treatments, or on the other side of their treatments and trying to figure out what to do or where to go. I want to help others get through their journey. That's where the BeYOUtiful community comes in. BeYOUtiful is a celebration of life, no matter where you are in your journey. To me, you're BeYOUtiful in every moment throughout the highs, the lows and everything in between. There's still a bright future ahead of your diagnosis and I am here to help you find it.

Words of Wisdom

First of all, attitude is gratitude. That's it, just plain and simple. You don't have to have cancer to feel like crap. You don't always feel like crap when you have cancer. But you do have to have the tools and the clarity to move yourself forward. That's where I come in.

By Tammy Rader

Join the community at BeYOUtiful.health

BeYOUtiful Beyond Your Diagnosis by Tam:

BeYOUtiful: https://beyoutiful.healthinstagram.com/tammy.rader73

Tammy Rader is a contributing and 2X International Best-Selling Author of The Cinderella Monologues and Live Life in W.O.W! Nuggets of Wonder, Openness and Wisdom and is an emerging speaker.

She is a Cancer survivor and Mentor, focused on guiding those with cancer through and beyond their journey. Having been diagnosed just 39 days apart with both Breast and Rectal cancer, Tammy is now a "Thriver," who finds resilience with the help of humor, practicing mindset and having gratitude.

Tammy is the Founder of ***BeYOUtiful Beyond Your Diagnosis (by Tam)*** *and has Nurture Mail (cards), Journal, program, group and one-on-one talks. She loves the simple little things in life, like going for walks in nature, the sound of laughter, ladybugs, unicorns and flip flops.*

Overcoming Anxiety and Guilt

By Corey Poirier

Tell Us Your Story

I have multiple stories. One for me is that I battled hypochondria, and generalized anxiety for about four years of my life. Most people know what anxiety is, but hypochondria is something not everybody would necessarily know. The hypochondria part is basically when you hear about a disease or read about a disease, and then you develop the symptoms of that disease. I know exactly when it started. I was in a waiting room in Edmonton, and I read about Michael J. Fox coming out about the fact that he had Parkinson's. He was really young, but it came out that he had had it for around eight years; since his late 20s. I don't know what triggered inside my head, but a couple of days later, I started having tremors and I started having different things that I'd read about in that story. But the wild part is when you're going through that, you can't actually recognize that you just read about it and you're actually mimicking the disease. You don't make the connection that this is all in my head. I remember thinking that I was developing the same thing that Michael J Fox has. That started a series of me going into the hospital for testing for whether it was MS or Parkinson's, and the doctor putting me through various tests and then saying you're fine, there's nothing wrong. Then because I was still feeling something, I discovered a new disease and then I developed the symptoms. This became a cycle for years, and the best way I can describe it is that it was like living in these little compartments and my life was just minute to minute. I was in this little war inside my head about what was going on. But I couldn't see that tomorrow was going to be a better day; I was stuck in this loop. That was probably one of the most challenging times in my life. Another story is quite a different story. I was raised by a single mother, and I'm an only child and my mother is an only child, so we have a really tiny family. I was really close to my grandfather, and he taught me how to drive, and how to be a man; he was my surrogate father. I didn't live in the same town anymore, but I was home visiting. My mother told him that I was going to stop by and see him, but I had a meeting to go to so there was no way I could go see him that morning. I went to the meeting, and then I drove home. A week and a half later, my cousin knocked on my door. He just showed up and said, "I'm so sorry," gave me a piece of paper, then just walked back out to the car. I opened the paper and it just said, "Call your mom." When I called my mom, she told me that my grandfather had passed. For three months, I was destroyed inside thinking about the fact that my grandfather died thinking I was gonna go visit him and then didn't bother, even though my grandfather would never have thought that way. I never told my mom about that for months, but it ate me up inside that I didn't go see him, and that would've been the last moment I would have had with him. Even though I didn't do anything wrong, it really wasn't anybody's doing. But it's funny how inside we beat ourselves up. I struggled with that for four or five years. The first three months, I thought about it all the time. Whenever I thought about him, I would feel this immense guilt.

How Did You Get Through This?

For me, it's actually a different answer for both scenarios. With the anxiety and hypochondria, I had a blessing that came into my life. I got tricked into performing stand up comedy one night, and on that stage, I bombed; I was terrible. I didn't get any laughs, but I survived. I went back the next week, and I kept going back. What I noticed is people at work started asking if I'd met somebody, because I had a different feel about me, a different energy and a jump in my step. It was then that I started discovering that stand up comedy had become a passion. That evolved into speaking and other things, but what I discovered is what I call Vitamin P - passion or purpose. I would say that day, I took Vitamin P for the first time. Once I discovered a passion, it was as if I took a vitamin that works, and all of a sudden, the anxiety and hypochondria just disappeared, and it has never come back since. What I believe is that you can't have a pessimist and an optimist equally living in the same body, it's hard to be either fully positive or fully negative. What I think happened to me personally was that I was a pessimist. I was very negative for those four years. But when I discovered that purpose, that was like taking my passion pill, and it basically got rid of the negativity. The takeaway from this is to find a purpose, or something that you were designed to do. Figure out what your purpose is, and then start living on purpose. For me though, it was an accidental one, so it wasn't really a mindset thing. So, knowing what I know now, I would tell somebody to develop a mindset and put the positive energy in before you need it. Before I ran into those four years, if I would have been filling myself with positive energy and positive affirmations, and it wouldn't have probably ever happened in the first place. So, this one involving my grandfather is a little tougher because by the time that happened, I was already Mr. Positive. I was already past the anxiety and hypochondria, and it was more just a trigger whenever I thought about it. One of the things that I did was, I started writing down all the times my grandfather told me how much he cared about me in his own way, without saying those words. I also started thinking about proof that he wouldn't have been mad at me for not showing up. At the same time, I started depositing more positive thoughts each time I thought about it. I was trying to replace the negative thought that happened every time I thought about it with a positive thought.

The other thing I did is I thought about the thought itself, not the situation. Was it going to be something I would remember a year from now? If I'm not going to remember a year from now, then why am I wasting my today over it? To summarize, the big takeaway from that is I started practicing reframing. Instead of thinking he would have been so disappointed that I didn't show up, I thought about the fact that he always told me to live fully and not live with regret. So, now I'm living with regret, and the guy who always taught me not to live with regret is the guy I'm regretting something about. I thought about the fact that he wouldn't want me to hurt myself over and over again over something like that. None of it is necessarily meant to be easy, but the tools are there to do it. And in my experience, if you do the work, it works. I think I had to feel those feelings because if we don't have pain, how do we know what happiness is? I was meant to go through that to know how to reframe it and become a better version of myself. So, I don't regret going through that. I'm actually grateful because I got to learn another side of me and learn how to get through something that isn't easy.

What Would You Tell Someone Going Through a Similar Experience?

Sometimes it's hard to come up with one specific answer, because there are multiple things. I would tell them that you have to go through this. And to be honest, it's similar to asking the question, "Would you get into a time machine to go back if you could make a specific change?" People usually say no, because they now know that going through that was necessary for them to become the person they are today. I would also say, "I know it doesn't feel like it now, but this is a necessary part of your journey to becoming a great person. You're going to become a person that will help other people in the future, then we'll see why this was important to go through as part of your journey. It won't be easy, but buckle up and brace yourself, because it's worth the ride."

There is no challenge I can think of where I would say change this or wish this away. This is a necessary part of your journey to become the person later in life that you are okay with.

What do You do Now and How Can People Work with You?

We ultimately help experts become instant experts. We help people level up and in a lot of ways it's in the eyes of the client that wants to hire them, so we help them get those credentials. For example, we might help them:

- Become a bestselling author, that's our compilation book series
- land a TEDx talk
- get on our blu talks stage
- get on our podcasting platform

But ultimately our goal is to help them realize these types of achievements and then showing them how to leverage their achievements. We help people to get more clients, to get increased fees for their services, those kinds of things. So ultimately, we're helping experts to level up, and for people that are just starting the journey, help them to demonstrate to their clients that they are or they are becoming an expert in their field. We do this in quite a few different ways, so if people wanted to connect with me to find out more about that, I would just ask them to reach out and to book a call at www.speakonblu.com.

Words of Wisdom

When I discovered my calling or my purpose, everything in my life changed. So what I would say to people is it's worth the work to find the thing that you're called here to do. And what I've also discovered is that for those that don't have a passion yet, my experience is that finding a passion is the gateway to finding your purpose. So, when I say that's the gateway, what I mean is, I found that most people don't discover their purpose until they have a passion that they're already doing. So, for example, until I started speaking - which became my passion – I didn't know why I was doing stuff like that, or why I was here.

When I discovered speaking that's really when I discovered I was here to try to create positive ripples for other people. Do the work to find a passion that may ultimately lead you to finding your purpose. The combination of those two things, in my experience, will help a person become successful personally and professionally; more than any other thing I've discovered.

By Corey Poirier

https://blutalks.com/

ThatSpeakerGuy@gmail.com

www.CoreyPoirierMedia.com

A Journey of Resilience: From Medicine to Venture Capital

By Anish Kaushal

Tell Us Your Story

Anish's life took an unexpected turn when he embarked on a path that defied his initial aspirations. As a young student growing up in Canada, Anish had always envisioned himself becoming a doctor. It seemed like a natural choice, given his inclination towards science and math, as well as the influence of his family members who were involved in medicine. With dreams of donning a white coat and saving lives, Anish set his sights on prestigious medical schools. Fortuitously, Anish had the opportunity to apply to universities outside Canada, and he was accepted into the renowned University of Edinburgh and the University of St. Andrews in Scotland. The allure of studying abroad, combined with the impressive reputation of these institutions, excited him. Full of enthusiasm, Anish ventured to Scotland at the tender age of seventeen, ready to immerse himself in the world of medicine.

The initial years of Anish's medical education were exhilarating. He diligently pursued his undergraduate studies, thoroughly enjoying the medical courses and finding them intellectually stimulating. Anish excelled academically, earning a first-class honors degree and proving his dedication and competence. As he progressed into the clinical phase of his education, where he worked directly with patients in hospitals, he anticipated a continued sense of fulfillment. However, a pivotal moment arrived during Anish's second-to-last year when he returned to Canada for a four-month rotation. It was during this period that he experienced a profound shift in perspective. The routine of going to the hospital, treating patients, and witnessing their recovery failed to ignite the passion he had anticipated. Anish realized that despite his achievements and the support of his family, he didn't truly enjoy the life of a doctor. A sense of unease and dread accompanied his daily routine, casting doubt on his chosen path. Adding to the challenges, Anish received disappointing news regarding the Canadian board exams he had taken. Though he hadn't failed the exams outright, he had fallen short of the required score to be considered for residency programs in Canada. It was a devastating blow, as Anish had worked tirelessly, amassing a remarkable track record throughout his academic journey. Suddenly, his future in medicine seemed uncertain, and he faced an unexpected year-long hiatus with no clear direction. Determined to explore alternative paths, Anish sought guidance from individuals outside the medical field. Conversations with professionals in investment banking and consulting opened his eyes to the possibility of pursuing different career avenues. The idea of leaving medicine began to take shape in Anish's mind. However, his parents, recognizing the value of completing his medical education, presented him with a fair ultimatum: he had one year to explore his options, but if he didn't find a suitable alternative, he would have to return to medicine. With the clock ticking and a year of uncertainty ahead, Anish embarked on an arduous journey of self-discovery. He applied to a master's program in the UK as a temporary fallback plan, but he soon realized that real-world experience and securing a job held more promise than obtaining another degree. Despite encountering countless rejections and unanswered applications during his relentless job hunt, Anish remained undeterred. Driven by an unwavering belief in himself, Anish decided to take matters into his own hands. Armed with determination, he researched the venture capital industry—an area previously unfamiliar to him. Inspired by his father's suggestion, Anish reached out to 75 of the world's top venture capital firms specializing in healthcare. Sending emails to each firm, he hoped for even a single positive response. The response rate was predictably low, but Anish's perseverance paid off. One group extended an invitation to interview for an internship opportunity. Anish approached the interview with tempered expectations, his past failures weighing heavily on his mind. However, to his astonishment, he was offered the position just days before he was set to embark on the master's program, he had previously enrolled in. This unexpected opportunity required him to relocate to Amsterdam, where he worked for the corporate division of Merck, one of the largest pharmaceutical companies globally. Anish's journey exemplified the embodiment of courage and resilience. Overcoming rejection, self-doubt, and parental concerns, he dared to carve his own path. The summer of uncertainty tested his resolve, and moments of despair threatened to erode his confidence. However, he found solace and inspiration through motivational videos that reminded him of the importance of perseverance.

Anish's story serves as a testament to the power of persistence and the impact of reaching out to others. He encourages aspiring individuals to cast their nets wide, to explore various avenues, and to connect with people who may be willing to take a chance on them. By refusing to succumb to setbacks and embracing the notion that all it takes is one person to believe in their potential, Anish exemplifies the transformative nature of unwavering determination. As Anish reflects on his journey, he recognizes that the road less traveled often leads to unexpected destinations. By embracing the unknown and defying societal expectations, he discovered a sense of fulfillment that eluded him within the confines of traditional medicine. Anish's story continues to inspire, serving as a reminder that when courage and guts converge, remarkable opportunities await those willing to chase their dreams. Anish's remarkable journey from medicine to venture capital was marked by determination, resilience, and a deep desire to follow his true passion. It all began when he found himself halfway through his medical studies in Amsterdam, only to discover that he wouldn't be able to secure a job there. This realization forced him to reevaluate his career path. With the looming prospect of returning to medicine if he couldn't find an alternative, Anish was determined to explore other options. He embarked on a relentless pursuit, reaching out to venture capitalists around the world, engaging in countless conversations, and researching every opportunity that crossed his path. After several months of perseverance, Anish received three final round interviews with venture capital firms—one in San Francisco, one in Germany, and one in his home country, Canada. Having spent seven years away from Canada, he felt a strong pull to return and contribute to the burgeoning startup scene there. Choosing to seize the opportunity, Anish decided to join the Canadian firm. Little did he know that this decision would shape his future in ways he couldn't have anticipated. Starting with no initial funding, Anish witnessed the firm's growth firsthand, eventually managing a staggering $500 million in healthcare investments. It was a remarkable journey from the humble beginnings of a startup. Reflecting on his four-year anniversary at the firm, Anish realized the impact he had made. He had been there since the early days when the company was still in its infancy, and he had played a pivotal role in its success. His excitement and passion for the venture capital space remained unwavering as he continued to relish his work.

What Advice Would You Give Someone Going Through the Same Thing?

Anish acknowledged the difficulty and shared his insights. He emphasized the importance of designing a well-thought-out plan of action and investing time in research. Whether transitioning to law, as in Kelly's example, or any other field, Anish believed in taking a stepwise approach. He encouraged individuals to identify the necessary steps, research the target field, and connect with experts and professionals for guidance. To overcome the initial resistance from parents or spouses, Anish stressed the significance of showing them the plan of action. By demonstrating commitment and showcasing the effort put into exploring the new path, individuals could alleviate concerns and garner support. An open and honest conversation about personal happiness and fulfillment was essential to bridge the gap. Anish understood the fear of feeling like time had been wasted, but he stressed that the skills acquired in one field were often transferable to others. Drawing from his own experience, he highlighted the value of a medical background in his venture capital career. The ability to research, communicate, and work diligently were universally sought-after qualities that he had honed through his medical training.

Words of Wisdom

Anish's final words of wisdom were simple yet profound: "Keep going, you're doing great." He urged individuals to maintain resilience, keep moving forward, and give themselves credit for the progress made. Anish believed that perseverance and self-belief were key ingredients for overcoming obstacles and achieving personal fulfillment. As Anish's story reached a wider audience, his message inspired countless individuals to reflect on their own lives and consider the possibility of change. His unwavering determination and the impact he had made in both medicine and venture capital served as a testament to the transformative power of following one's true passion. The tale of Anish's journey from medicine to venture capital would continue to inspire others, serving as a reminder that life is too precious to be spent in a career that doesn't align with one's deepest aspirations. With his books set to be released, Anish was poised to share his wisdom, experiences, and poetic expressions with the world, paving the way for others to embark on their own transformative journeys.

By Dr. Anish Kaushal

Dr. Anish Kaushal is a venture capitalist, doctor and writer. Originally from Toronto, Canada, he spent six years studying in Scotland, getting a first-class degree in medicine from the University of St. Andrews and his MD at the University of Edinburgh. He then joined the healthcare venture capital world in Amsterdam working for M Ventures, the corporate venture fund of Merck KGaA and most recently in Canada, working for Amplitude Ventures, one of the largest healthcare funds in the country. He's spent the last several years in his spare time reading non-fiction and blogging, all of which you can find on his website https://www.anichexperience.com/. He's a MENSA member and was recently selected on the Peak's 2023 Emerging Leaders in Healthcare.

Rediscovering my Passion and Purpose by living my best D.A.S.H.! Daring to Achieve a Successful and Happy Life!

By Patti Stueland

Tell Us Your Story

Ever since I was six years old, I always knew that I wanted to be a teacher and that's exactly what I did. Right before my fiftieth birthday, my dad succumbed to his five-year battle of cancer, and I started noticing that I really did not seem to have that passion and purpose that I had throughout my 30 years of teaching and coaching athletics. I'd heard that there was depression that ran through the family, but I prided myself on my positive mental attitude. About three months after my dad had passed away, I thought I was having a heart attack, and I did something that you should never do… I drove myself to the emergency room at our local hospital. After three days in the hospital, I learned that my heart was fine. What they figured out is I had suffered a massive panic anxiety attack. They felt that it was all due to the depression and grief I was experiencing from the passing of my dad, because my dad had been the main man in my life. From there, I thought about how I was going to move forward. With my mom, we decided to get into a grief group, but my thinking was I was doing it for her. I wasn't doing it for me because I didn't need counseling for grief (so I thought). Until I started noticing that I was withdrawing from everything. I could barely get myself out of bed. I didn't want to go to work. I didn't want to interact with anybody, I didn't want to talk to anybody. I spent a couple of weeks in bed, which was highly unusual for me. It didn't really worry me too much until one morning I woke up and there was this voice in my head that said, "you know what? If you didn't wake up tomorrow, nobody would care". Immediately I got on the phone to call my doctor because I thought there was something wrong. The receptionist said I could see the doctor in about two weeks. I said to her, "You do not understand, if I do not get in to see him today, I may not be alive tomorrow." She then said, "the doctor can see you in two hours; he'll work you in." When I get there, they hand me this clipboard. I can tell from the questions that they're asking that they think I'm crazy or they think that I am depressed. I can't be depressed! My life's foundation is based on P.M.A. (Positive Mental Attitude)! From that visit, I not only found out I was depressed, I also discovered that I had zero estrogen in my system, so that was not helping. I discovered that depression is hereditary. My dad and my grandmother both suffered from it. Whether I wanted to admit it, I was someone who was suffering from depression, and I had found ways to cope with it all my life without really realizing that is what I had been doing. With that depression diagnosis and everything else I was experiencing at the time was teaching me the following… I was not inspired to teach anymore! I knew I still needed to go at least five more years before I could retire. Those last five years were a struggle. I was going to have to "fake it till you make it". Then two years before I decided that I was going to retire, I realized I needed to start doing something to inspire myself. I needed to change up my routine and do some things for myself. I finally realized I had been so busy taking care of everyone else, that I forgot to take care of myself. Time to make myself a priority! I joined some classes at our local junior college. I took a beginning piano class, and I learned how to play the piano. Now, of course, I'm 30 years older than anybody else in the class. Did I care? No! It was the very first time that I ever did a class for my pure enjoyment. Up to this point in my life, all the classes I had taken were for my teaching credentials and classroom management. It was all related to my job and nothing that was for my personal enjoyment.

I also took an introduction to drawing class at the junior college and a woodshop class at the high school I was teaching at. In the woodshop class, I learned all the basics, and I started making these incredible things! I was starting to refill my cup! I had been so good about giving and giving and giving, I was forgetting to fill my own needs. Once I started to get my life back on track, people began to say, "you can't retire; you're back on course again, you're ready to go." What they didn't understand was the reason I was doing well and feeling good about teaching was I knew it was going to be my final year. I knew this was the end of my public education career and I knew I was going to go all out and put it all out there on my terms! A month after my final school year had ended and July 1st arrived, that was the morning that I realized I was no longer an official staff member of the Apple Valley Unified School District. I remember thinking for about 30 seconds… "What the heck did you just do? What are you going to do now?" For the first time in my entire life, I did not know what I was going to do next.

I didn't put any pressure on myself but decided to let God and my Christian faith guide me. For my entire life up to this point, God had never let me down before, and he wasn't going to start now. I felt like it was really him that placed it on my heart that it was time for me to close that door of teaching and that he had another door for me to open; I just didn't know at that time what was behind the next door. One Sunday morning, I came across an item in the newspaper about being a certified life cycle celebrant. I thought that sounded interesting, so I went back to school for a year and now I officiate at weddings and funerals. Why did I decide to officiate funerals? A year before my dad had passed away, he'd asked me if I would officiate his funeral. I told him I'd never done that before, but if that's what he wanted, that's what I'd do. I wanted to be totally prepared, and a month before he passed away, I asked my dad if he would like me to share his celebration of life service with him? His response to me was…"

I would love that”. When I was done sharing what I had written for his service, he said, “that's exactly what I wanted.” After the service, I realized it had planted a seed for me to know that I had been given a gift. I was busy with my new officiant business when COVID hit, and the world kind of slowed down and stopped, including weddings and funerals. I thought, what am I going to do? Once again, God spoke to my heart and reminded me about my number one retirement goal of selling my house and traveling the United States full time in my motorhome. For the past four years now I’ve been doing just that! I am seeing incredible things, eating delicious new foods, and I meet the most amazing people! I hear their stories and find out about their backgrounds and the things that they do. Those are things that inspire me, and I hope that my story also inspires them. In January 2022, I happened to be once again pondering what it was, I wanted to do with the rest of my life? I happened to come across a virtual summit and one of the sessions I signed up for was to become a motivational speaker. It planted the seeds that made me think, wouldn't that be awesome to do! It had always been a desire of mine. But I thought well, I'm 61 years old, that ship has sailed. But listening to the presentation made me realize that I'm not done. I can still do that if that's what I want to do. During 2022 I created my business, “Pathways with Patti.” Because of my life and all the different pathways that I've been on, it was time to take all of this knowledge, all this expertise from all these people that were my mentors, coaches, people that inspired me, and family and friends, and pay it forward. They had paid it forward to me, so it was now time to do the same for those who were crossing my path. Through “Pathways with Patti”, that's really what I have gotten to do. Through my signature message that I call ‘living your best dash’, when I go and I speak to people, one of the first things I ask them is, “How many of you can say that you're living your best life?” People usually say “Yeah, I'm living my best life.” Then I say, alright, let's take it one step further, “How many of you are living your best dash and I'm not talking about the dash for cash or the 50-yard dash." I'm talking about when you go to a cemetery and you look at that headstone, and you see a date of birth, and a date of death, there is what looks like to many people that insignificant, tiny little line in between those two dates. That little, tiny line represents a person's life and their time here on Earth. It tells the story of their life. So, what will your dash represent to others when people see it? Is it going to be a dash that represents a life of oh, I should have. oh, I could have, oh, why didn't ... Or does your dash represent a life of oh my gosh, that Patti, you know even though she retired, look what she did. She became a life cycle celebrant. She did this and she did that. What is your story going to be?" Unfortunately, in America, there's this underlying message that once you get to middle age, that's it. It's either golf, pickleball, knitting or crochet. And there is nothing wrong with that because I do all those things. The point that I work on helping people realize is this: if you still want to have other passions and purpose in your life, there are ways to still make it happen! It's never too late to create a legacy that you can be proud of!!! Through my "Pathways with Patti," I'm doing motivational speaking. I also started my "Rediscovering Your Passion and Purpose with Patti" podcast. I got to write a chapter in a book that went to the number one Amazon Best Selling list which is crazy. I had a couple of magazines ask if I would write an article for them. I enjoyed the writing process so much that I started writing a weekly newsletter that goes out to my list. The feedback that I'm getting is inspiring and continues to ignite my passion and purpose! In January, when I was asked to be a part of the "Impact 2" book (each chapter is about a motivational acronym), I was asked, do you have an acronym for the word Dash? I didn't at the time, but quickly created an acronym that I am very proud of! My acronym for the word D.A.S.H. is: "Daring to Achieve a Successful and Happy life"! That's exactly what I'm doing; that's my message. What I'm paying forward to other people is helping them to find out what their passion and purpose is. Along with that, helping them to create a plan, take that plan, and put it into play. You are only limited by your imagination on what you can do. Here I was just twelve years ago, going from lying in bed for two weeks and having a thought in my head that said, if you didn't exist anymore, nobody would care, to this day of incredible life experiences! I want people to open up their minds to know whatever your age is, you're only limited by your own imagination of what you can do and your determination and your willingness just to try some things. Does everything always work out for me? No, it does not! Is everything positive for me? No, it is not! I had an incident where I was going to go camping in the Sierras and through a whole series of unfortunate events that happened, God was telling me perhaps I shouldn't go to the Sierras. Even after this series of unfortunate events, I continued to go and when I was about five miles from the campground, I watched my motorhome burn to the ground with everything in it! All I had were the clothes on my back and the two people that were with me unharmed. After all that I had just been through, I chose to stay with my family for that week and camp. At the end of the week, I'm sitting on the end of a pontoon boat with my six-year-old niece. She hasn't understood why Aunt Patti's motorhome is not in this empty space at the campground. While we were fishing, she turned to me and she said, “Aunt Patti, your motorhome has burned to the ground, and you have nothing!” I looked at her and said, “You know what? You're absolutely right! But even though that happened, we had a wonderful time together this week haven’t we!” What was I going to do, go home and just be sad and somber about the fact that I lost my motorhome and everything that was in it? Yes, I was upset, and I had PTSD for a while, but the bottom line was… nobody died, and nobody got injured. Things can be replaced, people can’t. From that horrible incident, that was the positive in this situation. That's what I focused on, people cannot be replaced, but things can be! That's the way my brain works. When a bad thing happens - and they are going to happen - how am I going to look at that incident and turn it into something where I learn from it, I grow from it, and I move forward.

Where Do You Find the Gift and Then Move Forward?

A lot of people just see how tragic life can be, but I acknowledge that tragedies happen, what am I going to do about that? For me it all has to do with my faith in God. He is my foundation. It's ok to have a pity party, just don't pitch a tent there and stay! I want to experience as much of life as it has to offer me! There will be times that I fall. That's going to be a part of the journey. In order to take on the adventure of life, get up, dust yourself off, learn from it, don't look back and move ahead!

How Can People Work with You?

If you want me to speak, I am more than happy to come and speak to you virtually or in person. I talk about a variety of topics, for example, one of my talks is about the whole thing that happened with my motorhome; that's a whole signature talk that I do right there. I also speak on "Living Your Best D.A.S.H.: Daring to Achieve a Successful and Happy life." My website is www.pathwayswithpatti.org and you can go to that website and sign up for a free 30-minute zoom chat with me - a "Patti Chat" is what I like to call it. We can talk about where you are and what are the things that you would like to do, and we can start talking about your passion and purpose. Also, if you have a story where you've overcome some challenges and yet through all of those challenges, you have rediscovered your passion and purpose, I want you to be a guest on my podcast show called, "Rediscovering your Passion and Purpose with Patti". You can reach out and contact me through my website to be a guest on my podcast. You can also email me at Pastueland@gmail.com. I also have a six-week course that I do live on zoom. We do exactly what I say, we look at where your life is. Where is it that you believe that you want to go? Once they know where they want to go, I work with them to create a plan. Once we've created the plan, they put it into play! A couple of my favorite sayings are: "make it a great day or not, the choice is yours" and, "Attitudes are contagious; is yours worth catching?" I want my attitude to be contagious in a positive way. I also want each day to be the best it can be. I want that for other people as well, because it makes a big difference in what way and direction your life moves in. My motto has been since I retired, "life's an adventure, enjoy the journey," and that's what I'm doing.

Words of Wisdom

My final words of wisdom are that if you have a heart that is beating, and you are breathing, you still have an opportunity to make a difference in this world. You can still create a legacy that you can be proud of at any moment in time. It's all about making that choice. If your choice is to live the very best life you can with passion and purpose, reach out to us; we are here to help you, because YOUR LIFE MATTERS!!!

By Patti Stueland

www.PathwaysWithPatti.org

Pstueland@gmail.com

Patti Stueland is living her best life! Retired after teaching and coaching in public education for "35" years, Patti continues to reinvent her life's dreams, goals and ambitions. During her retirement over the past seven years, she has become a Life Cycle Celebrant officiating weddings and funerals. She has also become a full time R.V.'er, traveling around the United States in her motorhome. She loves to share her adventures of travel on her social media sites! She is now on a new journey as a motivational / inspirational speaker. Her business "Pathways with Patti" offers workshops and a six week online personal transformational program called "Pathway of Hope: A New Beginning."

Reinventing Your Life

By Sheri Berke

Tell Us Your Story

I spent over forty years working in large companies, and I had gotten very good at dealing with office politics and all of the things that you needed to master in order to be successful at getting your function performed. I was excited about retirement, and I'd been looking forward to it for a long time. I thought I had a list of great things to do. I was going to go back to school and do some of those classes I skipped the first time. I had gone through an accounting and business management track, so there was no time for those fun courses. I wanted to go back and take fashion design, photography and those creative, playful things. I planned to spend time with my husband, travel, read, and garden. I was excited about the prospect of spending years doing this. But it was only about a year before I started to get bored and depressed.

I'd been taking these great classes, and they were fun and exciting. You can only take so many classes, go so many places, and read so many books before the joyfulness starts to dim. I thought retirement was going to be this wonderful experience, but something was missing, and I wasn't quite certain what it was. One day I was flipping through social media, and I came across a couple of quotes talking about dreams and your purpose in life. I'd pretty much completed all of the dreams I'd set for myself. After you achieve a dream, there's excitement because you did it. Then there's a let down because your project is finished and now what? I didn't feel I had a purpose that was pulling me forward any longer and began to question what my next step was. I had spent decades adding value to companies and helping other women develop their careers. Now that my career was over, what

I realized was I still had a lot of amazing years left. I needed to get back on track with dreaming and setting some new powerful goals; I needed to continue to add value and to work with others. I wasn't totally sure exactly where to begin. I had come across a woman who was a coach, and I started to work with her. She helped me along the path to put together a new direction for my life. I was able to continue my journey to make a difference, to work with women, and to support them in creating a new life for themselves using my experiences. Along the way, I became an entrepreneur. At a time in life when many people were wrapping up and winding down, I was ramping up. What I started to feel was this sense of excitement. I had dreams again. I was working with other women who were coming alive and formulating new dreams.

While I had traveled, there were new places I was dreaming of going to. I wrote one book that became a bestseller: *Everything I Learned About Life I Learned on Vacation*, and have almost finished my next book, a workbook: *Plan A Vacation, Plan Your Life*. What I really learned is that when you have a purpose and a dream, you'll keep going no matter what your age. You may be on the precipice of your best dream ever.It took a lot of courage for me to do that and to become willing to admit that maybe things weren't perfect. To have the willingness to make changes in my life, and to admit that I didn't necessarily know the next steps or the path forward, and to seek help. All of these things took a level of willingness and courage in order to move forward. It's been an amazing time of my life, but at the same time, there were scary times. I was doing things that were new and different for me, outside my comfort zone. Stepping out created a major change in my life. No matter what your age, you can find people who are doing what you aspire to do, and they can provide inspiration.

What Would You Say to Someone in This Position?

I would tell them that life continues to be a new adventure. This is where you go back to basics, and you refine your skills to create a new future. Go daydream and imagine what things could be like. Recapture those days when you were a little kid, and you were fearless. You wanted to do one thing one day. You'd work your way through the whole scenario, even play acting it out, or talking to other people and getting some great information. Maybe what you'd discover was that your scheme wasn't exactly the way you wanted it, so you'd refine it again and again. Or you'd decided it wasn't going where you wanted it to and go do something different. There was a lot of self-discoveries about your unlimited boundaries, who you were and what those deeply buried desires were. Then you'd surround yourself with other people who supported you in your journey; you don't have to do it alone. Or maybe you did do it alone, that only made you stronger.

What Was the First Step You Took That Helped You Get Through It?

I had a passion for knitting and spent a lot of time in a knit shop. When you sit and knit, you also share about what's going on in your life.

I'd talk about the photography course I was taking and shared some of my images. The owner of the knit shop asked me if I would consider taking photographs of some of her product offerings for her marketing materials. She'd pay me for it. I said "Yes!" I started to take pictures for her, and she was using them. I thought, maybe I could do this for other people. Maybe I could make a business out of this, but I'd never run a photography business, so I went looking for someone who had that experience. Someone who had that expertise and could teach me. I found it online. I started to walk the path of a professional photographer, and what I discovered is that rather than taking pictures for other people, I loved to do picture taking for my own entertainment.

While I also photographed a number of weddings, and got paid for them, I decided that wasn't for me. What I enjoyed was the thrill of working with people and supporting others to fulfill their dreams. That started me on the path of looking at what might be next, and it's evolved. I love working with women and now I do it as a Reinvention Expert and a Dream Fulfillment Mentor. It evolved from saying yes to an opportunity to take a few pictures and get paid for them. From that I found a new and different career. I have a new passion, and it's helping others to attain their life's dream. People get put off by the thought of having to go through a change, and they'd rather stay stuck in a rut than burst out of it and do something that they're passionate about. It does take courage and guts in order to do that. It may not be something that everybody around you endorses. You may have to find a new group of people who support you. Who are saying, "Yes, you can do this." It's that fear of change that keeps people stuck and sometimes they need help.

What Do You Do and How Can People Work With You?

I help people unleash that dream buried secretly in their heart. I support them in the process of navigating the road to fulfillment. I act as their cheerleader. We celebrate successes, and I support them if they have to pick themselves up after they've suffered a setback. We work together creating the path to identify their dream, and then we work to make it real. I've discovered that sometimes the process of doing that seems a little daunting, but I've developed a process where I work with them as if they're planning a vacation. They may easily plan a vacation and go through all the steps prior to getting ready to go on vacation. Then they'll go on it, come back, and be excited about how fabulous it was. Then we apply that process to their dream and make it real. I learned about life by going on vacation. I've developed that theme more in my next book, which is a *Plan a Vacation, Plan Your Life Workbook*. I support my clients to translate vacation planning into creating a life project, such as buying a house, getting a new career, or going back to school. Something they may be passionate about.

Words of Wisdom

One of my favorite sayings is "What you think about you bring about. You can do it."

By Sheri C. Berke

sheri@sheriscw.com

https://TheReinventionPlaybook.com

How to Plan Your Life Like You Plan a Vacation:

https://bit.ly/plan-yr-life

Sheri is a TEDx speaker, bestselling author of Everything I Learned About Life I Learned on Vacation, dream fulfillment mentor, and coach. While she has been leading change innovation projects in companies of all sizes in her entire career, her favorite reinvention is facilitating the personal transformation of individuals to match their dreams. She holds an MBA from the University of Southern California and is also a former Certified Public Accountant (CPA). As an innovation change manager in business, Sheri impacted small businesses and well-known companies such as Boeing. She regularly uses her intuition for results and works co-creatively with the

Universe to develop solutions and support transformation. Her vision is to support professional women over 50 who feel they have lived out all their dreams and believe their best years are behind them.

We hope you enjoyed our stories. To listen to the live interviews and hear stories from other inspirational people, go to our podcast at: https://linktr.ee/ggcshow

If you would like to be in the next Grit, Guts and Courage book, reach out to Kelly at: BookKellyToSpeak@gmail.com

Author Interviews On Spotify
Episode7 - Resilience in Recovery: Overcoming Adversity with ADRIENNE TICHY
Episode 28 - Unveiling Resilience: ANNA DITCHBURN'S Journey of Healing and Empowerment
Episode 3 - The Journey with my Mom and her Sidekick, Dementia with BETTINA MARIA
Episode 16 - Overcoming Fear and Pursuing Your Dreams with CHUCK ANDERSON
Episode 26 - Betrayal - Let it Empower You with DEBORA J. HOLLICK
Episode 13 - From Tax Lawyer to Alphabet Expert: DIANE DEVENYI'S Inspiring Story
Episode 6 - The Language of Play with DINALYNN ROSENBUSH
Episode 19 - The Power of Angels and Intention with DONNA FAIRHURST
Episode 21 - Overcoming Trauma, Finding Purpose, and Helping Others with DR BARNSLEY BROWN
Episode 15 - Collecting True Friends: The Key to Success & Happiness in Business & Life with ELIZABETH DUNCAN-HAWKER
Episode 2 - Grief is Love: Changing the Narrative on Grief with HEIDI DUNSTAN
Episode 23 - Finding Your Purpose: Navigating Fear and Regret with JENNIFER JAYDE
Episode 25 - From Ballet to Energy Healing: Defying Expectations and Embracing Purpose with JESSY MORRISON
Episode 12 - From Isolation to Inclusivity: DR. JONATHAN KING's Journey of Breaking Barriers
Episode 18 - Zone of Potential: Making the Most of Your Opportunities with KARIN SCHULTZ
Episode 10 - From Darkness to Resilience: A Journey of Transformation with KEN COURSE
Episode 22 - Trusting Your Gut and Finding Your Zone of Genius with KIMBERLY CROWE
Episode 29 - From Adversity to Empowerment: LABAN DITCHBURN'S Journey of Healing and Inspiration
Episode 9 - Uncovering Your Superpower Through Spiritual Transformation with LAURA STAISIUNAS
Episode 8 - Unleashing Creativity Through Intuition: A Conversation with Psychic Artist LOIS WARNOCK
Episode 11 - Surviving Childhood Trauma and Thriving: A Personal Journey with MARY BLACK
Episode 14 - Overcoming Loss and Living Life to the Fullest with MICHELLE ABRAHAM
Episode 27 - Unleashing Resilience: Embracing Challenges, Making Bold Decisions,& Pursuing Clarity with MIKE C-ROC
Episode 20 - Finding Courage and Purpose in the Face of Adversity: The Story of RACHELLE BABLER
Episode 5 - The Power of Resilience in Storytelling with TAMMY GROSS
Episode 4 - Finding Laughter and Gratitude in the Face of Cancer: TAMMY RADER's Story
Episode 46 - Overcoming Anxiety and Guilt: COREY POIRIER's Journey to Positive Living
Episode 39 - A Journey of Resilience: From Medicine to Venture Capital with ANISH KAUSHAL
Episode 34 - From Darkness to D.A.S.H. - Defying Limits: PATTI STUELAND'S Remarkable Journey of Resilience and Renewal
Episode 47 - Reinventing Your Life - SHERI BERKE
https://linktr.ee/ggcshow

Bonus Interviews On Spotify
Episode 17 - Overcoming Adversity and Building a Successful Business with CHRISTINE ROTHDEUTSCH
Episode 24 - Unleashing Your Inner Power: Transforming Fear, Embracing Resilience, and Shining Brightly with CHERYL STELTE
Episode 30 - A Tale of Grit, Guts, and Gratitude: The NICOLE TUXBURY Story
Episode 31 - Navigating Law and Life Without Sight: The Inspiring Story of ERIN EDGAR, the Blind Lawyer
Episode 32 - Commanding Your Life: Empowering Young Men to Take Flight Towards Their Dreams with JEREMY STOKER
Episode 33 - Unleashing the Power Within: DEBBIE BRYAN'S Extraordinary Journey of Resilience
Episode 34 - From Darkness to D.A.S.H. - Defying Limits: PATTI STUELAND'S Remarkable Journey of Resilience and Renewal
Episode 35 - Navigating Through Anxiety and Finding Truth: A Conversation with AMANDA YOA
Episode 36 - Unlocking Passion: BRAD WALSH's Leap from Corporate to Photography
Episode 37 - Unmasking Identity: A Journey from Closeted Athlete to Diversity Advocate with CHRIS ROLLINS
Episode 38 - DEBRA KASOWSKI'S Manifesto: Embracing Challenges through Commitment and Courage
Episode 39 - A Journey of Resilience: From Medicine to Venture Capital with ANISH KAUSHAL
Episode 40 - Uncharted Resilience: The ROB DUBIN Journey to Happiness
Episode 41 - Embracing Authenticity with TIFFANY PATTERSON
Episode 42 - Resilience Unleashed with ALAN SIMBERG
Episode 43 - Embracing Wisdom Within: COLLEEN JORGENSEN's Journey of Acceptance and Courage
Episode 44 - Unveiling Infinite Horizons with MASHA PAVLOVA
Episode 45 - Courageous Entrepreneurship with MICHELLE NEDELEC
Episode 46 - Overcoming Anxiety and Guilt: COREY POIRIER's Journey to Positive Living
Episode 47 - Reinventing Your Life - SHERI BERKE
Episode 48 - Surviving the Stampede: STUART ELLIOTT
Episode 49 - From the Edge: Overcoming Inner Demons with MITCH CAMMIDGE
Episode 50 - Beyond Sexuality: A Journey of Self-Discovery with SANDRA BELLAMY
Episode 51 - Rising from the Abyss: BRENDA SHELDRAKE'S Journey of Redemption
Episode 52 - Grit, Guts, and Courage: Overcoming Life's Challenges with ALVIN LAW
Episode 53 - Resilience in the Face of Tragedy: A Survivor's Journey with JENNIFER TAKAGI
https://linktr.ee/ggcshow

Made in the USA
Columbia, SC
05 March 2024

32716955R00124